By Gail Sforza Brewer

*What Every Pregnant Woman Should Know: The Truth About
Diets and Drugs in Pregnancy,* with Thomas Brewer, M.D. *(1977)*

The Pregnancy-After-30 Workbook, editor *(1978)*

An Italian Family Reunion Cookbook (1982)

The Brewer Medical Diet for Normal and High-Risk Pregnancy,
with Thomas Brewer, M.D. *(1983)*

Nine Months, Nine Lessons (1983)

By Isaac Cronin and Gail Sforza Brewer

The Complete Pregnancy Nutrition Cookbook (1983)

By Gail Sforza Brewer and Janice Presser (Greene)

*Right From the Start: Meeting the Challenges of Mothering
Your Unborn and Newborn Baby (1981)*

By Julianna FreeHand

Elizabeth's Dream (1983)

A Seafaring Legacy (1981)

The Westchester Treasure Hunt Tour (1980)

Breastfeeding

Breastfeeding

Text by Janice Presser and Gail Sforza Brewer

Photographs by Julianna FreeHand

 *Alfred A. Knopf   New York   1983*

THIS IS A BORZOI BOOK
PUBLISHED BY ALFRED A. KNOPF, INC.

Text copyright © 1983 by Janice Presser and Gail Sforza Brewer
Photographs copyright © 1983 by Julianna FreeHand
Illustrations copyright © 1983 by Nicky Gelfer
All rights reserved under International and Pan-American
Copyright Conventions.
Published in the United States by Alfred A. Knopf, Inc., New York, and
simultaneously in Canada by Random House of Canada Limited,
Toronto. Distributed by Random House, Inc., New York.

The authors would like to thank Professor Irwin H. Kaiser, M. D., of the
Department of Gynecology and Obstetrics at Albert Einstein College of
Medicine, Bronx, N.Y., for reviewing the manuscript prior to publication.

Library of Congress Cataloging in Publication Data
Presser, Janice. Breastfeeding.
   Bibliography: p.
   Includes Index.
   1. Breast feeding. I. Brewer, Gail Sforza.
II. FreeHand, Julianna. III.Title.
RJ216.P68 1983   649'.3   82-48736
ISBN 0-394-52414-4

Manufactured in the United States of America
First Edition

To

Esther Friedman Presser,

Camille Sforza Rose, and

John Taylor Hand

Breastfeeding

For many months now you have been caring for the new life within you. The child you have sheltered in your womb will soon be in your arms.

You have decided to breastfeed, following the tradition of mothers since the beginning of time. Like them you want to give your baby the best possible start in life—the perfect nourishment, the continued warmth and comfort of your body, and a tangible expression of your love. Breastfeeding is the most personal gift you can give your child: more than just your milk, it is the gift of yourself, your substance, your presence.

There is nothing to compare with the bond that joins a nursing mother and her child. It is one of the most complete and extraordinary relationships possible—at moments peaceful, sweet, urgent, trusting, sensual, trying, yet so often full of wonder: the essence of true giving and receiving.

When you think of breastfeeding, you think of yourself and the baby. But breastfeeding encompasses all those around you. It is a new way to love, but it is also a new way to live, a way that has proved itself over the ages to be in the best interests of you, your baby, and your whole family.

When you were very young, you learned most of what you knew about being a woman from your mother. You played dress-up in her clothes, experimented with her lipsticks and powders, mimicked her at work, used her tone of voice when you played house.

If you ever saw her pregnant with a younger sibling, you walked around —perhaps with admiration, perhaps with envy—with your own small tummy protruding in imitation. When her baby was born, you most likely were given a doll.

If you grew up where breastfeeding was the norm, it seemed natural to mother your doll by holding it tightly against your flat chest. If most babies you saw were bottlefed, then that was the way you fed your doll.

You may not be able to recall clearly that time of your life, but the messages you received then from your mother, your sisters, your aunts, cousins, and family friends live on in your memory. They influence the way you feel about your body, and they help shape the decisions you make as a woman.

As a little girl, your breasts, inside and out, were indistinguishable from those of little boys. Only with the onset of puberty did the wonderful difference start to be apparent. Your maturing ovaries increased production of female hormones, causing the area around the nipple, the areola, to swell with new growth. The inner network of ducts that would one day be essential to the feeding of your baby also proliferated.

Whether you were proud of your budding breasts or worried by them, they confirmed your approaching adolescence. Your first bra signaled to everyone that you were preparing to leave childhood behind forever. Your sisters and friends may have begun looking at you in a new way: as older, wiser, more experienced—even though you may have felt the same inside as always . . . just a little girl.

Hormones worked other changes in your body: the rapid transformation to an unmistakably feminine figure, underarm and pubic hair, and, finally, your first menstrual period. Throughout your young womanhood, your hormones ebbed and flowed, bringing monthly ovulation and menstruation, and cycles of fullness / growth / regression in your breasts.

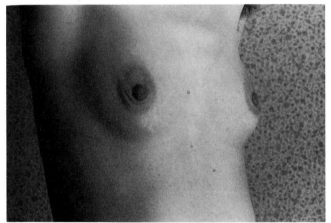

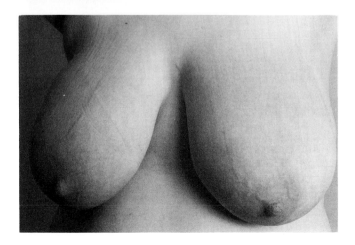

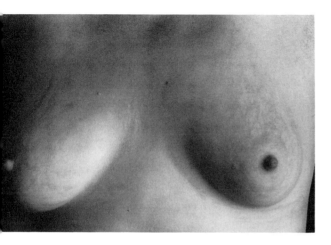

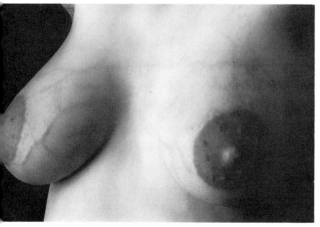

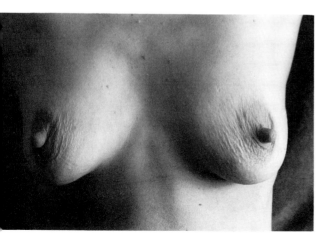

Eventually, you reached the full flowering of your womanhood. Now you are pregnant, and your breasts, once again under the influence of powerful hormones, accelerate in growth and prepare to make milk for the first time.

Long before the stirrings of your baby cause tiny ripples on your abdomen, your breasts tingle, feel warmer, fuller, heavier. Suddenly your bra is much too small and your breasts may be so sensitive that they are painful to touch. These sensations may even be the first suggestion that you have conceived.

No matter how they look or feel— large, small, pendulous, perky, soft, firm, even-textured, or lumpy—your breasts' inner workings are the same as those of all other women: they are milk-providing glands surrounded by cushions of fat cells. All breasts have the biological capability of secreting milk in the process called lactation.

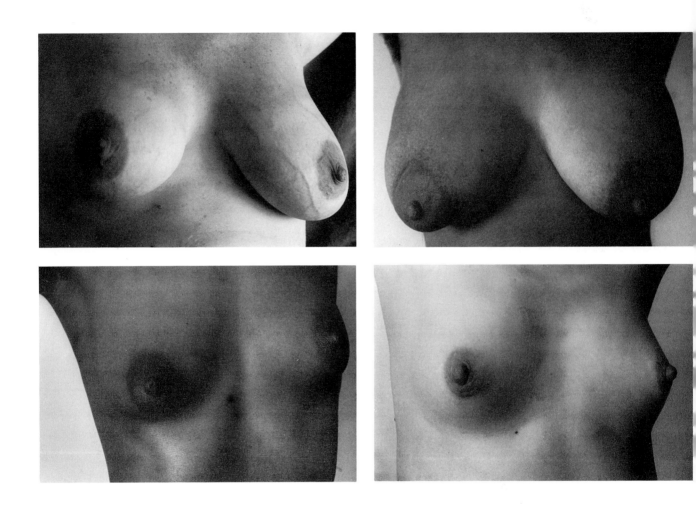

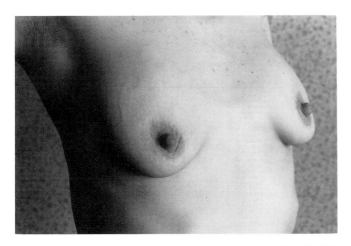

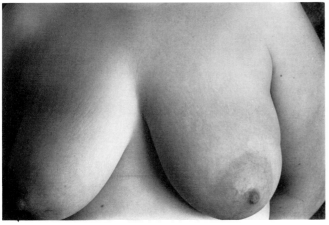

Much is made in our culture of the size of a woman's breasts. We receive conflicting messages about them, and learning when it is appropriate to display them and when they are to be covered is part of every girl's education. Breastfeeding rewrites some of these social rules.

Enjoyable breastfeeding comes about when you become truly comfortable with your breasts—able to handle them in private and in public when your baby requires it; able to cope with their larger size, different shape, and (for a time) unpredictable secretions.

As your pregnancy becomes noticeable, people again single you out for special regard. You have already started to be a mother.

Look closely at your breasts and compare major features with the photographs. You will notice several tiny openings in each nipple. Because we are so accustomed to bottles and commercial nipples with a single hole, this may be an amazing anatomical discovery.

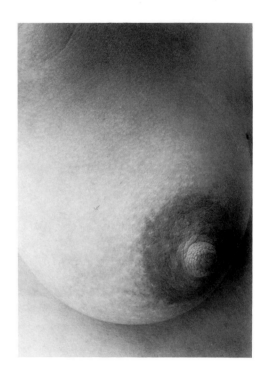

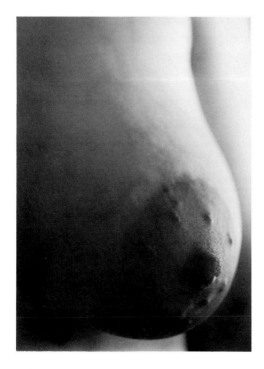

If you are past the midpoint of pregnancy, you may even see small drops of colostrum, the precursor of milk.

Pregnancy causes the pigment of your areola to darken. If your skin is very light, the new shade may resemble the color of toast. Women with brownish coloring may go all the way to black. Small bumps, called Montgomery's tubercles, appear around the areola. They continually secrete a creamy substance that invisibly lubricates and protects the nipple. This is why you do not ever need to use any lotions or creams on your breasts, nor any soap.

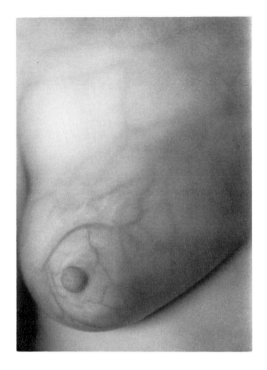

Circulation to your breasts increases dramatically during pregnancy, and a tracery of bright bluish veins becomes visible through your skin. Stretch marks may develop—red lines radiating outward from the nipple. These are due to rapid breast growth and fade into pale silvery streaks in the months after you give birth.

The skin of the breast also contains fine hair, oil glands, and sweat glands which contribute to each mother's unique smell. Your baby will be able to differentiate you from all others two days after being born.

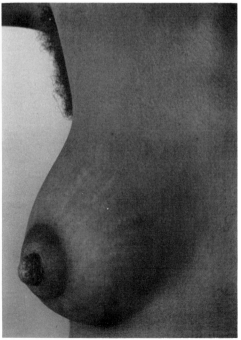

Most nipples protrude on stimulation, but yours may be flat or inverted, usually because of many fine adhesions that "tie" the nipple to surrounding tissue.

To test for inversion, simply run your fingers over your nipples. If they do not stand out erect but either pull in or stay flat, you may have difficulty getting your baby to start nursing. This is especially common at the very beginning when you have an overabundance of milk that causes the breast tissue behind the nipple area to swell and the breasts to become engorged. You may even be told mistakenly by someone who does only a quick visual check that you have inverted nipples that are unsuitable for breastfeeding. True inverted nipples are extremely rare; however, because they have been told so, many women believe that they have this problem and never even consider breastfeeding.

Even if your nipples really are inverted, they can be made functional for breastfeeding by gradually breaking the tissue adhesions around the areola with gentle traction over a period of several weeks and by wearing corrective milk cups.

To correct flat or inverted nipples, wear milk cups inside your bra for three to eight hours a day (depending on the degree of inversion) during the last four months of pregnancy.

Follow the instructions that are provided with your set. If your nipples have not everted by the time you give birth, continue to use the cups between feedings, discarding any milk that collects inside them.

To get the baby latched onto a flat nipple, arrange the baby in nursing position, then draw your nipple outward between your thumb and forefinger, twisting it gently until you feel it swell slightly. Immediately introduce it into the baby's mouth.

Milk cups are available for $3.00 a set from: Nursing Mothers' Council, Childbirth Education Association of Greater Philadelphia, 5 East Second Avenue, Conshohocken, PA 19428 (215-828-0131).

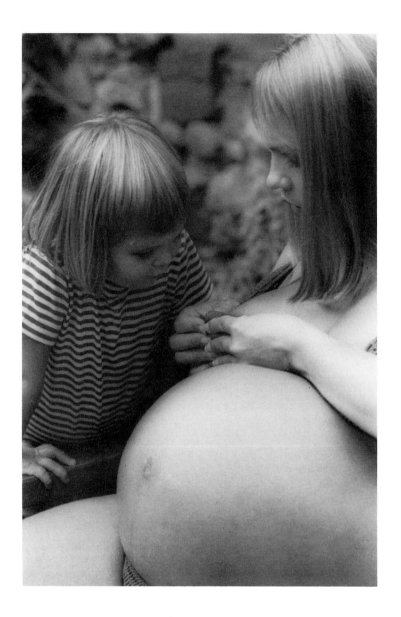

Most women have tender nipples for a time at the start of breastfeeding, the fair-skinned more so than the darker-complected. If you had spent your young womanhood in a part of the world where women go bare-breasted, exposed to sun and air as a matter of course, your early sensitivity to your baby's insistent suckling would be considerably lessened.

During pregnancy you can take some of the sting out of the first week of nursing by giving your nipples the kind of stimulation that layers of clothing deny them. This does not mean treating your nipples roughly—vigorously pulling, twisting, or rubbing them with coarse materials—in order to harden or toughen them. Nipples in good condition are elastic and resilient, yet still sensitive.

A dietary regimen that produces healthy skin is the basis for healthy nipples (see page 17 and Appendix, page 138, for specifics). Next add daily exposure to sunlight and air—the ideal is to sun yourself either outdoors or under a sunlamp (for no more than three minutes). At night, massage your nipples with vitamin E and gently tease them out with your fingers for five minutes or so. Pure vitamin E (not mixed with any other oil) can be purchased in capsules that need piercing or, better still, in a small bottle.

If you have delicate skin—susceptible to dryness, reactive to soap and perfume, easily sunburned—go braless as much as possible, or if you need to wear a bra, buy a nursing bra and wear it with the flaps turned down, in addition to following the above suggestions.

Your first breast secretion is colostrum, a food specifically for the newborn.

After the fourth month of pregnancy you may find flakes of dried colostrum on your nipples. Rinse with clear water as soap may be too drying for your skin.

Colostrum differs from mature milk, which gradually replaces it during the first week of breast-feeding. Colostrum is richer in amino acids—the building blocks of life—and contains antibodies that protect against various diseases. It also contains living cells, macrophages and lymphocytes that assist in cleaning out the baby's intestinal tract and facilitate the digestive process. Immunities you have built up or developed after inoculations to ailments such as polio, measles, mumps, and rubella are also transferred to your baby in colostrum, and will last for some time.

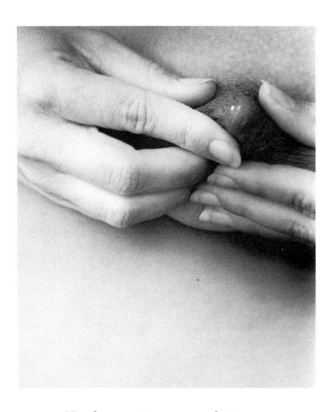

Hand-expressing some colostrum during pregnancy is another effective way to prepare your nipples for breastfeeding. Gently massage all areas of your breast, stroking from the chest wall toward the nipple. Then place your fingers on either side of the nipple, behind the edge of the areola. Using a scissorlike motion, bring your fingers together and apart several times in rapid succession. The clear drops that exude from the nipple are colostrum.

Do not worry if you cannot express anything. The colostrum is there, ready to nourish your newborn, whose suckling is far more efficient than your fingers in drawing it out.

Your mate may have mixed feelings about the changes in your body, especially as they affect your lovemaking.

Many men appreciate your added voluptuousness, but nipples too sensitive to tolerate the pressure of a bra are unlikely to respond ecstatically to oral or manual stimulation by your partner. If you are still nursing an older baby, you may find the pain so uncomfortable that you decide to wean or reinstate your proven program for tender nipples: crushed ice packs applied after every nursing, vitamin E massage, air-drying, and extra sunshine. If your older baby is very dependent on your milk for much of the day's nutrition, keep reminding yourself that it's just the initial sucks that make you wince. The discomfort usually tapers off during the rest of the feeding.

Some women find the heightened sensitivity of their nipples a strong sexual plus during pregnancy: they are able to attain orgasm with breast licking, fondling, or sucking alone. Lovemaking may prove to be your preferred method for preparing your nipples for nursing, if your partner is willing to do your breast massage and nipple teasing for you. For others, the pain-pleasure combination reduces sexual excitement. Tell your partner what you are experiencing and realize that this extreme sensitivity may pass as pregnancy progresses.

Men vary in their reaction to finding colostrum or milk in your breasts. Your mate will not deprive the baby by having a taste.

having a premature baby, metabolic toxemia of late pregnancy, placental abruption, severe infections and anemias, or a Cesarean birth. Any of these situations could create medical emergencies that sabotage a mother's best attempts at breastfeeding. If you are intolerant to milk, you must substitute extra servings from the protein group on the food chart, e.g., more eggs, meat or vegetable protein combinations, and green leafy vegetables. Remember that a quart of milk contains thirty-two grams of protein.

Frequent nourishing snacks help you meet important nutritional requirements, especially in the latter part of pregnancy when the growing baby leaves little room for large meals. For the details of a medically tested diet to prepare you for breastfeeding and support lactation for as long as you and your baby desire, consult the Appendix (page 138).

Prepare good meals at home, take the time to enjoy your food if you work away from home, and do not be concerned if you gain thirty to forty healthy pounds or more on a sound diet. Your breasts alone may account for an additional three to four pounds, and the extra blood you need to serve the placenta, which transfers nutrients to your baby, adds another three to five. A great deal of fluid is also retained in your tissues, due to the high level of female hormones manufactured by the placenta during pregnancy.

An excellent diet during pregnancy is crucial to getting off to a good start with breastfeeding. If you satisfy your appetite with a wide variety of foods from the basic food groups—milk and milk products; meat, fish, poultry, eggs, and vegetarian equivalents; fruits and vegetables; whole grains— and if you salt your food to taste, a recent recommendation of the American College of Obstetricians and Gynecologists, you will significantly reduce your chances of

You may question your decision to breastfeed when you learn that others whose opinions you value do not share your enthusiasm.

If you were bottlefed, your mother may view your desire to breastfeed as implied criticism.

If your husband wants to share baby care with you, he may resent not being able to feed the baby.

If your friends had problems nursing their babies, they may discourage you by saying it isn't worth the trouble. They may even give you a bottlefeeding kit as a shower gift. Make light of it at the time. Just be sure to store it on your most inaccessible shelf at home!

Society's indifference to breastfeeding makes it all the more important that you locate some colleagues who share your philosophy of mothering. This should not prove too difficult since today more than half of all new mothers leave the hospital nursing their babies.

There is no lack of information about breastfeeding for today's mother. Hospitals, clinics, volunteer organizations, public health agencies, women's centers, and childbirth education classes are all doing the job of promoting breastfeeding as the most healthful way of nourishing new babies. Even companies that manufacture infant formula now publish booklets outlining the advantages of breastfeeding to mother and baby and giving basic instructions in breastfeeding immediately after birth. Much of the current emphasis on breastfeeding originated twenty to thirty years ago with mothers who wanted to breastfeed their babies but who found that society in general viewed bottlefeeding as the superior, "scientific" way of feeding one's infant. Reclaiming the art of breastfeeding as an essential part of the maternal cycle has been the goal of numerous organizations around the world. The success of these efforts culminated in the statement issued by the American Academy of Pediatrics in 1978 that endorsed breastfeeding as the preferred method of infant feeding.

In spite of all the current outpouring of information, you are still likely at one time or another to want to talk to another nursing mother—to find out how she handled some small problem you are having or which pediatrician she found who strongly supported breastfeeding. For this reason, you should contact your local childbirth group early in pregnancy to find out about breastfeeding support groups in your area. Some of these groups have regular meetings that mothers may attend with their babies and openly discuss various concerns. Other groups work on a mother-to-mother basis. Your counselor handles your questions privately whenever they come up— even at 3 a.m. when you can't get your baby to stop nursing and go back to sleep (you wouldn't dream of disturbing the baby's doctor at that hour!). Whichever way your local group works, it exists for the purpose of sharing with you the "tricks of the trade," the mothering skills that have helped many others through the often trying weeks when you and your baby are both new at nursing.

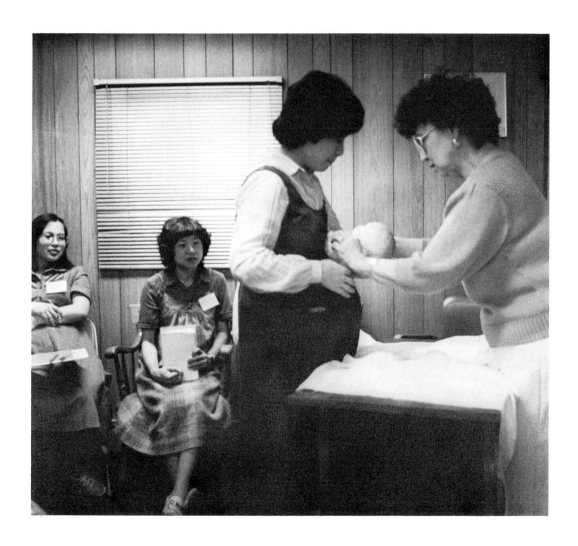

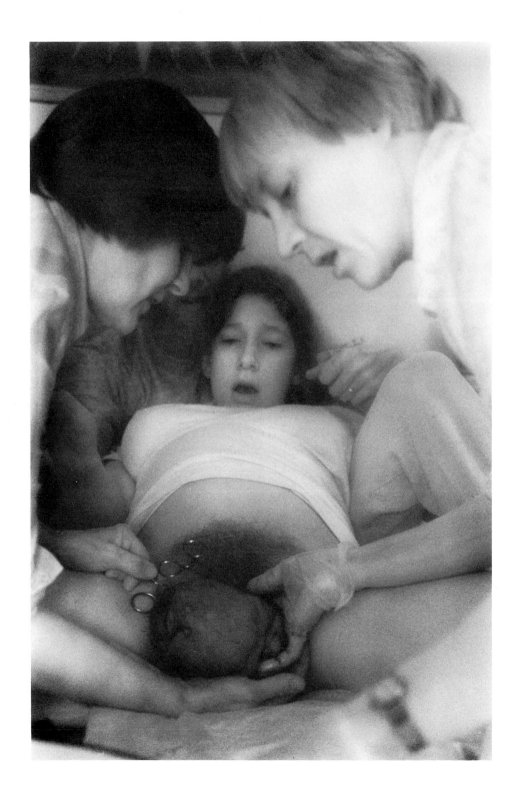

Intense uterine contractions propel your baby into the outside world and ready both of you for the first nursing encounter.

Before birth, your baby was held close and warm within your uterus, rocked by the motion of your pelvis and soothed by the sounds of your heart and digestive system. The foods you ate were automatically converted by your body into substances that passed through the placenta to nourish your baby continuously, and your body eliminated waste products for both of you.

If you were well nourished during pregnancy, your baby has never experienced hunger. Also, many babies have learned well prior to birth how to satisfy their sucking impulses by gumming their fingers.

If your labor has lasted more than twelve hours, you have probably gone for a long time without eating. This causes the supply of food energy stored in your liver to become depleted and your blood sugar level to fall. Nutrients circulating to your baby also drop off.

When your baby emerges, hunger, cold, and the urge to suck may all strike at once.

The child you have nourished from within for so many months is ready for nourishment from without. After the birth, your body continues to be your baby's best source of warmth, comfort, and food.

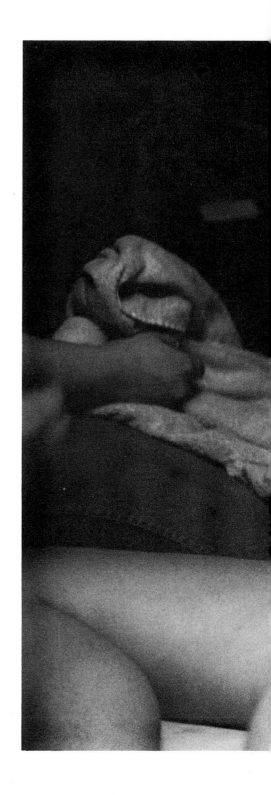

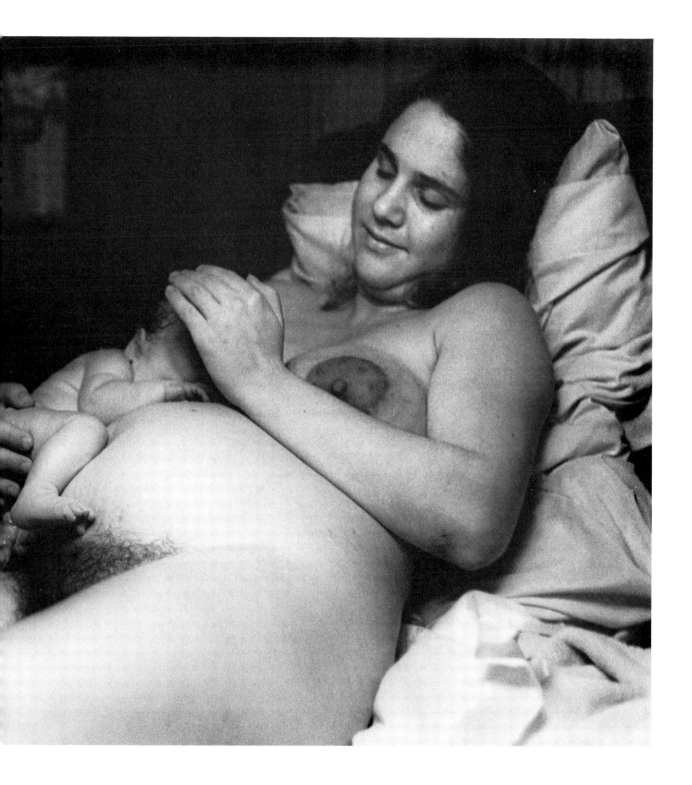

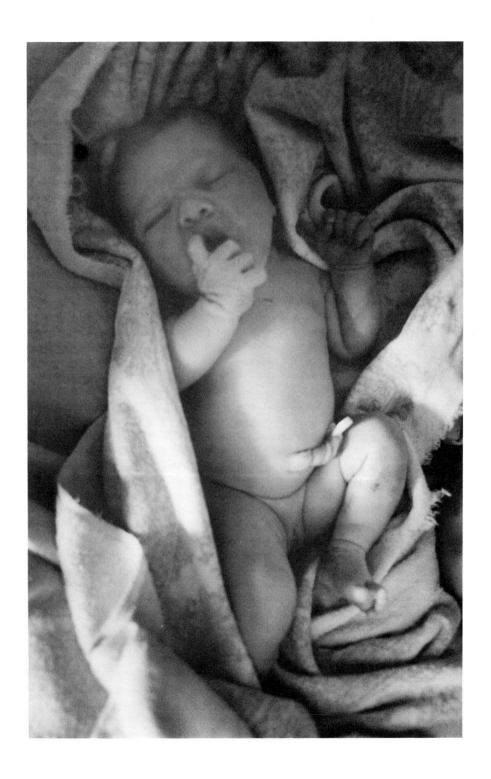

Your newborn's instinct is to search for your nourishing breast.

In the meantime, fingers—one or more—will do. This is a clear signal that your baby is primed to begin nursing. When your labor and birth have been unmedicated and the baby is in good condition, the sucking reflex generally reaches its peak within a half hour after birth. Delay in offering the breast may result in a baby who is somewhat more reluctant to nurse later on.

If the baby does not show readiness immediately after birth, perhaps the sights and sounds of the birthplace are temporarily of greater interest. Wait.

When the baby seems calm, introduce the nipple.

If your labor has been stressful, or there is some medical reason why the baby cannot be put to the breast at once, do not worry. Whenever you have your first opportunity for privacy with your baby, you will be able to initiate breastfeeding. Many mothers have given birth in hospitals where it is routine policy not to bring the baby to the mother for the first twenty-four hours and have still gone on to many months of rewarding breastfeeding.

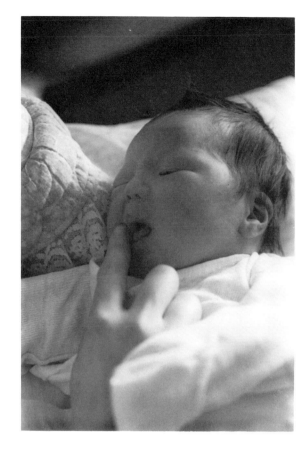

A series of inborn reflexes assures that your healthy, full-term baby will know how to nurse at your breast.

To initiate breastfeeding, hold your baby close to your breast, with the baby's head in the crook of your arm, or positioned directly opposite the nipple if you are lying on your side.

To guide the nipple into your baby's mouth, touch the cheek nearest your breast and continue stroking until your baby's head turns toward the breast. At the same time your baby's mouth will open and the "rooting" reflex will be activated. The baby's head may shake back and forth in tiny, urgent circles until making contact with the nipple.

Nurse as soon after birth as your baby is able and willing, then frequently—at least every two to three hours—thereafter. After each nursing, allow your nipples to air-dry before tucking your breasts back inside your bra (if you wear one).

To help your baby latch on and begin suckling, use your fingers to hold the breast back from the nose. This flattens the nipple slightly to conform to the shape of your baby's open mouth.

Support the breast from underneath with the remaining fingers of your hand. Your baby may grasp your pinky now, but will not be able to manipulate the breast for several months. As time goes by, you will become expert at moving aside your clothing and bra to give your baby access to the breast in any situation. You may feel awkward at first if your nipple repeatedly slips from your baby's mouth, but just keep reintroducing it, and after a few tries your baby should be successful.

Correct positioning of your baby will go far toward preventing serious nipple problems. Most of the areola should be inside the baby's mouth, between the tongue and palate. This way, the nipple is drawn up and held in the mouth by suction, while the baby's jaws move on the outer rim of the areola. The baby should not just be chewing on the nipple itself.

Babies nurse best when they are hungry. It is hard to interest a sleepy baby in the breast. In the first few days your baby may need more sleep. Don't disturb the baby's rest just because you think it is time to nurse. It is better to wait until the baby really wants to suckle and not try to force the issue.

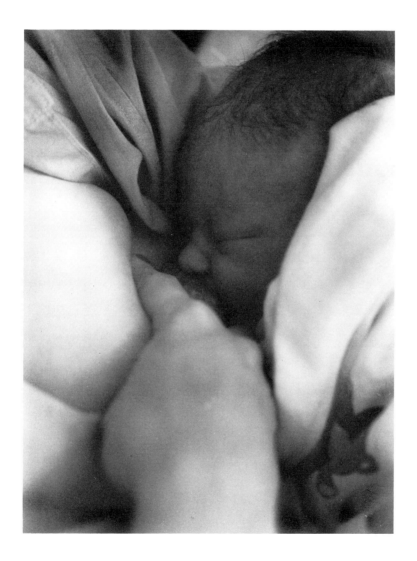

Babies have different "nursing personalities."

Some latch on immediately and nurse powerfully, then stop as soon as they are satisfied. These are the matter-of-fact nursers.

The snackers prefer to take in the main course for a few minutes, rest awhile, then come back for more, so the time spent nursing and holding your baby is greatly extended.

Others nurse so gently, it may be hard to tell when they are actually feeding from when they are near sleep and suckling just enough to prevent the nipple from escaping their mouth.

If your baby is a dawdler or if you want to see if the baby is still interested in more suckling, pull back a little without breaking the suction. If the baby has not really finished, vigorous suckling will be the response. Otherwise, your nipple will just slip from the baby's mouth.

Your baby's suckling naturally slows down as the flow of milk lessens during a feeding. This is your sign to transfer the baby to your other breast. Break the baby's suction by inserting your finger beside your nipple and loosening the baby's hold, then remove the nipple. Alternate the side you offer first so that your baby nurses equally on both sides and you do not become lopsided.

It is important that you offer both breasts to your baby at each feeding. If your feedings average fifteen to twenty minutes each and you switch breasts halfway through, your baby will obtain the richer "hind milk," the "cream" of the feeding, from the second breast. The baby's suckling at the first breast increases your hormones, and this causes your hind milk to come in. In the first seven minutes of a feeding, the fat content of your milk increases fourfold, from one gram per 100 milliliters to four grams per 100 milliliters, and then plateaus at the highest level for the duration of the feeding.

The second half of the feeding is therefore extremely important because your baby needs to obtain approximately 50 percent of all calories from these fats. In addition, fats are essential to the growth and optimal functioning of your baby's brain and nervous system. Fats are also required for the progressive gaining of weight, the healing of wounds (an important consideration if your baby has been circumcised), and the development of filled-out, satiny skin—a classic sign of the breastfed baby who is blessed with a well-nourished mother. Maintaining your pregnancy diet with its balanced supplies of fats, proteins, vitamins, minerals, and fluids will assure that you are offering your baby the highest quality milk available.

By the way, your baby's stool will be very different in color, consistency, and smell from that of a bottlefed baby. A breastfed baby's stool is bright yellow and creamy and has a slightly yogurtlike smell.

The best nursing routine is the one that suits your baby. You may not have a regular schedule for weeks, although many people still suggest that you not feed your baby more often than every three or four hours, no matter what method of feeding you are using. Your breastfed baby may require a feeding every hour either for physical reasons (stomach empty) or emotional reasons (wants your companionship). Both reasons are valid. Breast milk is so completely digested and with such ease that the baby is ready for more sooner. To make your baby wait another hour or two just because of a preconceived schedule ignores the baby's very real nutritional needs and is a primary cause of failure of the breastfed baby to gain weight appropriately.

Depending on the condition of your nipples, you may be able to tolerate nursing for twenty to thirty minutes out of every hour right from the start, but don't count on it. Generally, gradual buildup over a few days is less likely to cause you distress. Even mothers who have nursed before find that their nipples are tender as they begin to breastfeed again.

Expect some initial soreness and use crushed ice packs, vitamin E massaged into nipples, and sunshine to make them feel better—the same strategies you used during pregnancy to prepare them for nursing.

It is inadvisable to limit nursing time to less than five minutes on each breast in the beginning. Your baby will not receive adequate fluids or proper nutrition. Your initial soreness will be prolonged because the excess milk in your breasts will back up, causing engorgement and greater difficulty in getting the areola into the baby's mouth. This will result in the baby's chewing your nipple.

After the first rush of milk due to the hormonal changes that take place immediately after birth, your breasts will not make adequate milk without considerable stimulation from your baby's suckling. Nursing is a demand-supply interaction: the more your baby demands, the more your breasts supply, provided that you maintain your excellent diet.

Although you will be urged to offer your baby water (with or without glucose) from a bottle, refrain from this practice unless it is extremely hot weather and the baby needs extra water because of losses from perspiration. The best protection against dehydration is frequent breastfeeding whenever the baby needs it. Many babies nurse every hour round the clock for a week or two. They grow beautifully and your sore nipple problem is quickly past.

If your baby occasionally sleeps as long as five to six hours at night, it is not necessary to wake the baby up for a feeding. Babies wake when they are hungry.

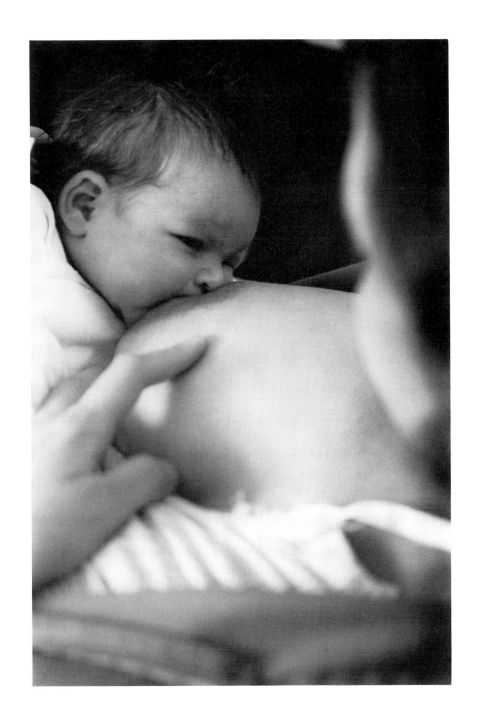

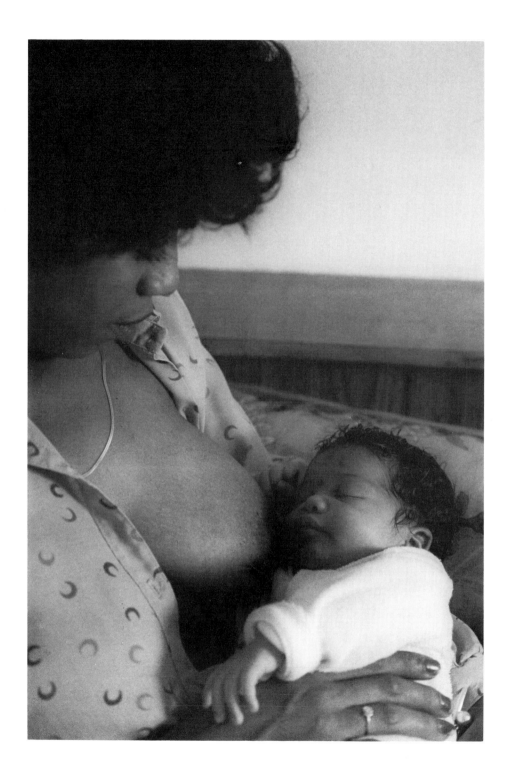

Most babies end the feeding session on their own. Satiated, they fall away from the breast, body relaxed, breathing calm, asleep in their mothers' arms.

Your baby may be one of those who still maintain a gentle suction on the breast, even though they are not actively working their jaws. At the most, you feel a flicker of the tongue a few times a minute. If you insert your finger beside your nipple to break the connection—and there is no protest as the nipple slips out—your baby, too, has finished nursing for the time being, every current need met.

If you are nursing with your baby in a carrier, your own movements as you go about your work after a feeding will usually produce a spontaneous burp from your infant; sometimes just adjusting the baby's position in the carrier will do it. If you are putting the baby elsewhere to finish napping, usually the pressure from being placed stomach down accomplishes the same thing. If your baby does bring up a big burp after being put down to nap and then wakes a half hour to forty-five minutes later and seems truly hungry once again, you have the sort of baby who needs burping after each breast so that adequate milk is taken in at each feeding and the baby doesn't mistake a tummy full of air for a tummy full of milk.

If your baby needs to be burped, banging vigorously across the back may cause the baby to spit up a good deal of milk in addition to bringing up the bubble. Instead, sit the baby upright on your lap, then bend the baby slightly forward at the waist and gently pat or massage the back. A little bouncing on the knee can accompany this. Sometimes just being raised up and gently placed across your shoulder will do the trick. If you have tried all of these methods and the baby has not burped, it may be that the baby does not need burping this time. Breastfed babies generally suck in much less air along with their milk than bottlefed infants do, so your baby may never require burping.

The effects of the nursing on you are also considerable. It makes you feel relaxed, calmer, in harmony with your baby. Your love bond with your child seems stronger than you could ever have imagined. These are the golden moments to savor, to anticipate, to recall for years to come.

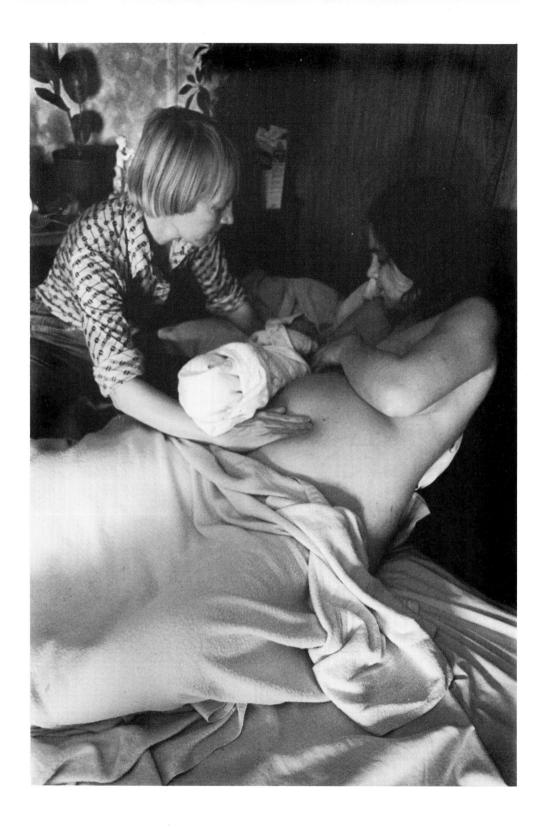

If your first nursing experience takes place within minutes after your baby is born, the stimulation of your nipples triggers the release of oxytocin, the hormone that is responsible for the milk ejection reflex in your breasts. Oxytocin also causes contractions of your uterus that result in the expulsion of the placenta (the third stage of labor). In hospitals where babies are not usually put directly to the breast, mothers may be given an injection of synthetic oxytocin to hasten the delivery of the placenta and to keep the uterine muscles tightly contracted, thereby minimizing blood loss from the open placental site. If your labor has progressed normally and you have required no medication, putting your baby to the breast eliminates the need for this injection in most cases. The baby's suckling (or any other form of breast stimulation if the baby is too interested in the surroundings to nurse right away) sets off waves of uterine contractions that help to protect you from postpartum hemorrhage; for this reason, it is very important to nurse often in the first few days after birth—and especially in the immediate postdelivery hours.

These contractions may not be obvious to you after giving birth the first time, but "afterpains," as they are often called, are usually more noticeable with the second or subsequent babies. Your physician may recommend a mild over-the-counter analgesic to take ten to fifteen minutes before a feeding to relieve any crampy discomfort. These contractions assist in the gradual return of your uterus to its pre-pregnancy size and position, a process called involution. Nurses will show you how to locate your uterus (now about the size of a grapefruit) to see if it has contracted and will teach you how to massage it to aid in your recovery.

After the emotional peak of childbirth, you may suddenly realize that you are hungrier and thirstier than you can ever remember being. If you are staying in a hospital, anticipate the kitchen being closed usually between 7 p.m. and 7 a.m. Bring your own celebratory meal and beverages in a second carrying case! At home, of course, you can toast your new arrival from your own bed.

Throughout the period of time that you breastfeed, the quantity and quality of your milk is dependent on your diet. Your appetite may zoom as your body continues to provide complete nutrition for your rapidly growing baby. Continue your pregnancy diet, adding additional nutritious fluids or water as you feel the need. It is good to drink a glass of something just before, during, or after each nursing session. Just as the nutrients your baby needs used to pass through the placenta before birth, now they must be obtained from your bloodstream by the milk-secreting cells in your breasts. Breastfeeding is the second half of pregnancy and it, too, makes large nutritional demands upon you. Fulfill them and you and your baby will have the best possible foundation for a satisfying nursing experience.

Avoid strong-smelling or -tasting foods (such as garlic or curry) to begin with until you are sure your baby likes these flavors as much as you do.

Do not be hard on yourself about shedding the extra pounds from your pregnancy weight gain. It took nine months to put them on; give yourself at least six months to take them off. Begin and keep up a moderate exercise program. Forty minutes of swimming a day, for instance, burns a pound a week! It is unlikely that you will lose all the extra weight until after you stop nursing because of the added fluids in the body.

Your baby's suckling at your breast stimulates the milk-secreting cells into activity. A network of nerves, glands, hormones, and the nutrients in your bloodstream are all necessary for the formation of milk as well as for its release in a process called the "let-down reflex," or milk ejection.

As your baby draws your nipple and most of the areola into the mouth, the tongue exerts upward pressure, compressing the breast tissue against the hard palate. The "fore milk," residual milk from the last feeding stored in the sinuses beneath the areola, flows in response to the negative pressure created inside the baby's mouth.

Nerve endings in the nipple and areola, stimulated by the suckling, signal the hypothalamus, a portion of the brain that plays an important role in regulating metabolism, which then influences the posterior pituitary gland to release both oxytocin and prolactin, hormones essential to milk production and ejection.

Oxytocin, the same hormone that caused your uterus to contract in labor, builds to a threshold level in your bloodstream that is able to affect your breasts within a minute after your baby starts to suckle. Oxytocin works directly on the cells that line the alveoli (milk-producing sacs), causing them to contract and eject newly made milk into the ducts leading to your nipple. You may notice this action throughout both your breasts as it gives rise to a tingly or prickling sensation. The breast not being nursed may leak at this time, since the inrush of milk often cannot be contained in the sinuses.

In the early days of breastfeeding, your let-down may be so abundant that your baby has difficulty keeping up with the flow of milk. Coughing, choking, and abrupt pulling off your breast may ensue. If this becomes a routine, express the mild by hand for a minute or two before you put your baby to the breast, introducing the nipple only after the initial surge of let-down is over. As the oxytocin level rises in your bloodstream, your uterus, too, is affected in a most predictable way: you again have uterine contractions that now aid in its postpartum return to a nonpregnant size and position. If you are wearing a sanitary pad, you may feel extra drainage while you nurse, a good sign that your healing after childbirth is progressing well.

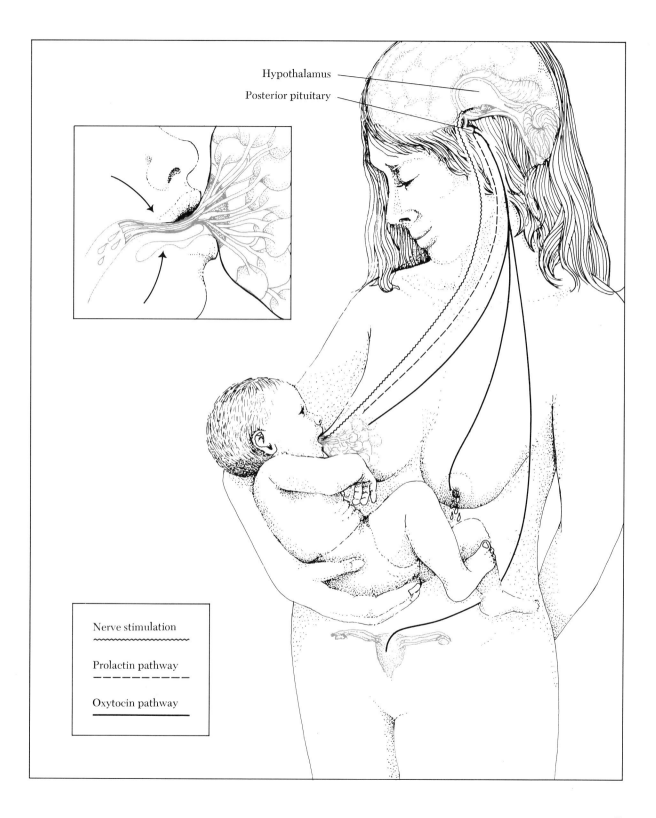

Hypothalamus

Posterior pituitary

Nerve stimulation

Prolactin pathway

Oxytocin pathway

Myoepithelial Cell at Rest

Myoepithelial cell

Duct

Gland cells around duct

Myoepithelial Cell in Contraction

Squeezing milk from milk-manufacturing cell into duct

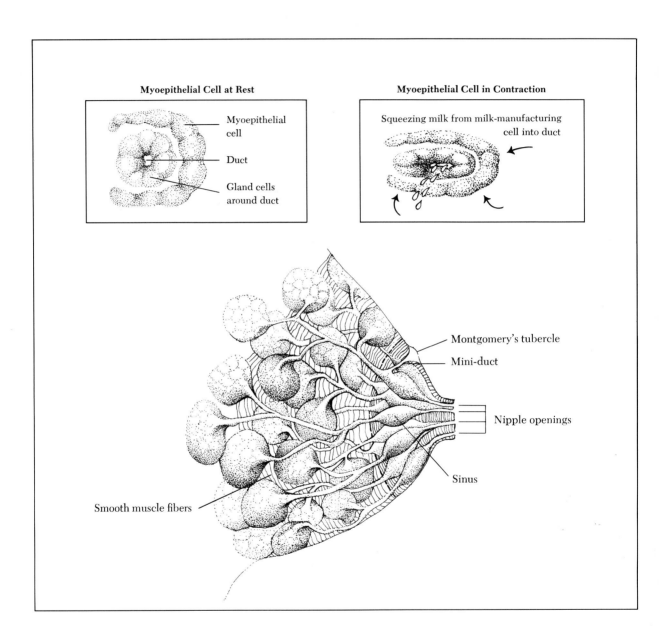

Montgomery's tubercle

Mini-duct

Nipple openings

Sinus

Smooth muscle fibers

The pituitary releases the hormone prolactin simultaneously with its release of oxytocin. Prolactin, like oxytocin, rises to higher levels the longer suckling takes place. Prolactin stimulates the milk-secreting cells lining the alveoli to combine selectively all the substances that make up your milk from the building blocks carried in your bloodstream. These cells also release fat droplets and proteins in higher proportions as the feeding continues, producing the richer milk, or hind milk, characteristic of the second half of each feeding. This heavier milk, with its concentrated nutrients, is then ejected into the ducts and on through your nipple to your baby, just as occurred with the fore milk at the beginning of the feeding. The longer your baby nurses, the more milk will be produced and ejected, assuming your nutrition is adequate for lactation, of course.

Even if your breasts feel soft after you have nursed for five minutes or so, this is not an indication that there is no milk left. It is just that the stored fore milk has been drawn off and now your baby is feasting on fresh, rich hind milk. Go another five minutes at least on the first breast, then switch to the second for as long as the baby wants to suckle. This insures optimal nutrition for your baby.

The let-down reflex can be inhibited by pain (such as sore nipples, a Cesarean incision, or an episiotomy wound on which you just sat down too hard). Anxiety or stress (especially worries about whether you are doing everything right in the hospital!) can also slow or halt let-down. Always try to get comfortable before you nurse, and if someone is around who makes you nervous, ask them to step away for a few minutes while you take care of the baby. As your self-confidence and skill increase, you will find yourself able to nurse anywhere you want and your let-down will be very reliable.

When planning for your baby's birth, check with your local childbirth education association or women's health center for information about all the available alternatives in your area: midwifery services, birth centers, early discharge from the traditional hospital obstetrics service. Though many institutions now offer extended periods of time during the day for you to share with your baby, many hospitals still insist on separating mothers and babies soon after birth. The mother is sent to a postpartum maternity floor and the baby to a central nursery to be cared for by others —and usually to be bottlefed even when the mother is trying to begin breastfeeding. Even in the most progressive hospitals, you may run into difficulties in keeping your baby with you during the night, or having the

baby brought to you whenever crying.

Schedules, for the most part, are what make a hospital run; however, you and your baby need to spend more than just half an hour together at intervals several hours apart. You benefit from your baby's frequent suckling because it reduces the incidence of cracked nipples and postpartum hemorrhage. Your baby continues to want a source of warmth, nourishment, and companionship. You and your baby have been together, as close as two different beings can be, for nine months. Neither you nor your baby is ready yet for separate lives. If your hospital is inflexible about nursery policies, and you and your baby are healthy, seek an early discharge; an overnight stay satisfies many doctors these days.

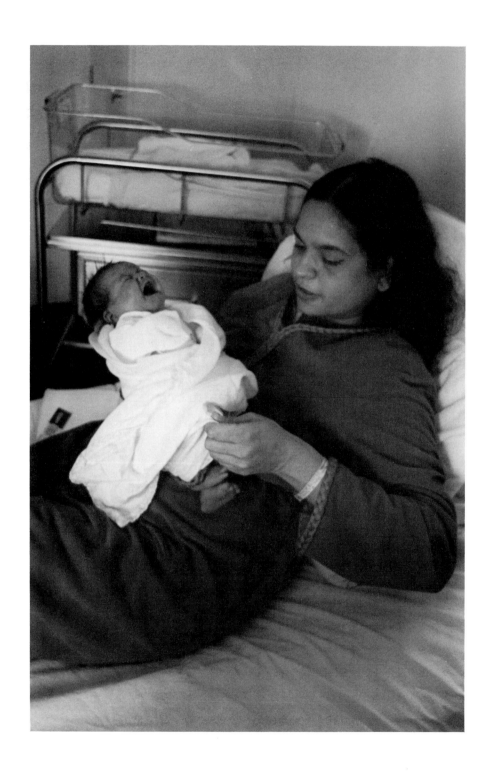

A popular in-hospital alternative to the central nursery is "rooming-in." The nurses, rather than caring for the baby the entire time, help you learn how to do it all: bathing, diapering, changing clothes, positioning the baby for breastfeeding, burping, napping, charting the baby's nursing activity and bowel movements, and taking the baby's temperature. If this is your first baby, a few days of rooming-in can give you confidence in your ability to care for your baby's day-to-day needs when you are home. You become closely attuned to your baby's needs so a little crying does not make you panic.

Should you feel tired or want to visit with family members, many hospitals now accept the baby back in the central nursery for the desired period of time. Others provide for rooming-in until nine or ten at night, then bring the baby to you to nurse every two hours or so until morning, if you wish. Discuss your preferences with your baby's pediatrician before the birth so specific orders about your baby's care will be waiting in the nursery before the baby arrives. A written order from your doctor is harder to ignore than your most heartfelt entreaties to have your baby brought to you during the night.

Generally the baby's father is not considered a visitor, subject to standard visiting hours rules. Fathers often arrive for breakfast, spend the day and evening, and, in some places, even stay the night! With this sort of rooming-in both parents come to know their new child much better before bringing the baby home.

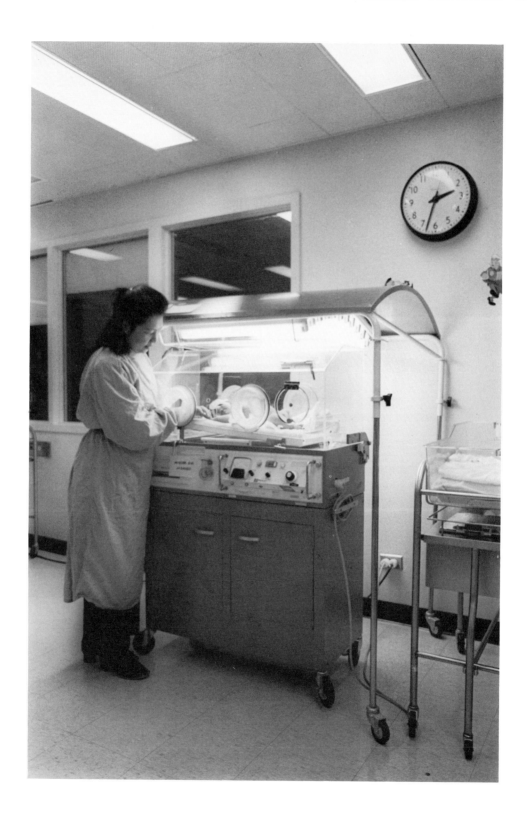

For some mothers the postpartum scenario is much different. They or their babies have problems that require intensive medical care. Even so, this need not rule out breast-feeding.

In fact, if a baby is born prematurely, breastfeeding is even more important than with a healthy baby. The mother's colostrum and milk are generally far more digestible than commercial formulas since the preemie lacks many digestive enzymes. The mother's milk may be pumped and given by stomach tube until the baby is strong enough to suck. The antibodies in breast milk safeguard the preemie from infection. If the mother cannot supply enough milk for her infant in the beginning, donor milk can usually be provided from a breast milk bank in the area.

It can take a very long time for a preemie to learn to nurse successfully, but the results are well worth the effort. If you must nurse in the intensive care unit, ask for a chair, try to find some private space, and be patient with yourself, your baby, and the staff.

Jaundice in the newborn, another common reason for admission to a special care nursery, is a yellowing of the skin caused by an excess of bilirubin (a byproduct of the breakdown of red blood cells). Jaundice can be a normal part of the baby's adjustment to life outside the uterus or an indication of a serious illness. Tests will be performed to establish what is causing your baby's jaundice. Often babies are placed under blue-spectrum fluorescent lights that simulate sunlight in order to reduce the bilirubin level. There is no need to stop nursing. In fact, the best thing you can do is to offer the breast more often since proteins contained in your milk are essential to the baby's excretion of bilirubin. Offering water at this time substitutes a no-protein fluid for fluid with the highest quality protein.

If your baby was born by Cesarean section, you, like many Cesarean mothers, may endow breastfeeding with even greater significance than women who gave birth vaginally. Especially if yours was an unexpected Cesarean and your mate was not permitted to share in the birth, you may well look to the pleasure and comfort of breastfeeding as a way to make up for the stress and separation you and your family have endured. Like all mothers, you want to take personal charge of your baby's care and feeding as soon as you feel fit.

Experienced Cesarean mothers who have breastfed successfully are your best resources for information and support. Also, more hospitals are employing nurse/lactation specialists whose job it is to assist mothers who need special help in getting off to a good start with breastfeeding. Some key strategies:

• Nurse as soon after surgery as possible. A regional rather than general anesthesia usually makes nursing possible within an hour or two after birth.
• Nurse lying on your side with a pillow across your abdomen to protect your incision from being kicked by the baby.
• When you are able to sit, a pillow across your lap raises the baby to breast height and, again, spares your incision.

• Arrange for your mate or another family member or friend to care for your baby in your room for as much of the day as you can negotiate.
• If you have been separated from your baby for twenty-four hours due to a medical problem, use the procedures for hand expression and breast massage that you learned during pregnancy to stimulate milk production even though your baby has not yet been put to the breast.
• If separation is going to last more than two days, begin using an electric breast pump at least every three hours to build up your milk supply.
• Get onto a high-protein diet as soon as possible, rather than the traditional postoperative course of nothing by mouth for twenty-four hours or more, to speed your healing and support your milk production.
• Accept needed pain medications, but try to minimize the use of those that make you feel drowsy or uninterested in your baby. The drugs most commonly used after Cesareans generally appear in breast milk in small amounts, and short-term administration (two to four days) usually has little adverse effects on the baby. A major exception is diuretics; they reduce the supply of breast milk by causing the body to eliminate large amounts of water, a necessary component of your milk.
• Contact your local Cesarean support group.

With frequent feedings, the colostrum in your breasts is gradually replaced by mature milk in one to three days after you give birth. If you decide not to give your baby water from a bottle in addition to colostrum, your milk will come in more speedily as your baby will want to be at your breast almost all the time. The baby is obtaining all necessary fluids from you this way and so will need to nurse much more frequently than the oft-cited two-hour interval for breast-fed babies. Babies permitted this unrestrained access to colostrum seldom lose much of their initial birth weight either. They are not being maintained merely on water "until the milk comes in." They are nursing vigorously on what lactation specialist Kitty Frantz, R.N., director of the Breastfed Infant Clinic, U.C.L.A. Medical Center, calls "supermilk"—colostrum, the very best nourishment available for the newborn.

Your baby's suckling causes a surge of activity within your breasts: they swell; they feel warmer than usual; they may begin to drip, leak, or spray; they resemble those of the buxom women painted by the old Dutch masters. You feel as though you are overflowing with milk—and you are! You can deal with the excess that drips while you nurse by placing a towel under the leaking breast. Well-nourished mothers usually produce an abundance of milk, just on the off chance that there is more than one infant to feed. Sometimes if the baby hasn't nursed for a few hours, your breasts may feel painfully hard. They stand out from your rib cage all by themselves, without the support of a bra. This is called engorgement.

To relieve engorgement, place a warm, moist towel around the breast. Repeat until the swelling goes down a bit, then massage gently to start the flow of milk. Now let your baby nurse.

Engorgement is very common with the first inrush of milk. Frequent nursing, at least every two to three hours around the clock, keeps engorgement to a minimum.

Engorgement can also occur later

in your nursing relationship if you must be away from your baby and miss one or two feedings. The less milk your baby is taking, the longer it will take you to become engorged under such circumstances. If you know you are going to be away from your older baby overnight, or you are detained and cannot complete your trip home because of bad weather, you can stave off some of the engorgement by sharply restricting your fluid intake. Do not restrict fluids with initial breast engorgement, however, as this will seriously interfere with the establishment of your milk supply. Use the warm towels when you feel yourself starting to fill up, and take a very warm

shower to stimulate milk flow even more. Hand-express as much milk as you can to soften your breasts and reduce your discomfort. Another breastfeeding mother who learns of your plight might even offer her baby to help you out if you are really in pain. One or two aspirin or similar analgesic may also be in order.

The next time you are considering leaving your nursing baby, think about whether it might not be easier all around just to take your baby with you. In the long run it might be less disruptive to have an infant at your business conference than to miss important parts of the meeting because you have to attend to your aching breasts.

Even if you have carried out nipple preparation faithfully during pregnancy, you may find that your baby's rigorous use of your nipples causes soreness in the early days of breastfeeding. You may even develop a cracked nipple if you do not take measures to prevent it as soon as you notice the soreness.

First, try to pinpoint the reason for the problem. Usually it is just from the normal nursing needs of your baby. However, any of these other situations could also be adding to your difficulties:

• The baby is chewing on the nipple because of incorrect positioning or because you are offering water in bottles. (The actions needed to obtain fluid from the breast and the bottle are very different, and this may be confusing to your baby.)

• The baby is not nursing often enough (at least ten to twelve times a day for the first few weeks is average), so you become engorged. When this happens, your baby cannot take the areola into the mouth and eventually starts to chew on your nipple.

• The baby is not nursing long enough to empty your breasts at each feeding; this also leads to engorgement.

• Thrush, a yeast infection that appears as white patches on an infant's mouth and tongue, has been transmitted by your baby to your nipples. Both of you will need antifungal medication prescribed by your doctor.

• You are using soap or salve or ointment on your nipples, a real assault on your skin which has its own natural oils for protection. Use nothing else but vitamin E on them and do not scrub with a washcloth.

• You are using breast pads with plastic liners to absorb any leaking milk. A simple cotton handkerchief folded into a square works beautifully and allows air to circulate. Change anything you are using as soon as it becomes damp, otherwise your skin will become puckered and easily broken.

• You are using a "bicycle-horn"

type of breast pump incorrectly and this has traumatized tissue with its excessive suction. (See page 104 for instructions on proper use.)

• You are wearing too tight a bra.

• You pull down your bra flap or move aside bra material hastily when it is stuck to your nipple, inadvertently stripping the topmost layer of skin.

• Your partner's unshaven face irritates your nipples because of too intense lovemaking. Ask for a gentler touch until your nipples heal.

Reject anyone's suggestion that you use a nipple shield. Using the shield prolongs soreness and lessens the stimulation needed for milk production. Instead, step up your nipple care program: air-dry after every feeding, apply vitamin E, expose them to sunshine if you can, apply crushed ice wrapped in a washcloth, take aspirin if you need it, and offer the sore breast second at every feeding so that your baby isn't quite so eager to latch on.

It always feels so wonderful to return home, especially when you bring home a new baby.

Planning ahead for the day-to-day necessities makes your homecoming enjoyable for everyone. Stock up in the last month of pregnancy on nonperishable foods, household supplies, and the baby's diapers and grooming essentials, and tame your closets so any helpers you have in your home will be able to find whatever they are looking for with a minimum of fuss.

Freeze meals ahead of time in preparation for the inevitable days in the next month when you will not be able to do much elaborate cooking.

To lessen the strain on all concerned, introduce your other children and pets to your chosen helpers before you have the baby.

Realize that you need help with the *household* (i.e., the cleaning, laundry, cooking, telephone answering, child escorting and supervising), *not with the baby.* Make sure your helpers understand this, too.

To take care of *you,* have your mate arrange to take parental leave for this first week so that the three of you alone can honeymoon together. If this is not possible, see if your mother can come, or someone else with whom you feel comfortable. If you have older children, include them in the baby's care whenever possible so that they do not feel excluded. Handing you diaper pins or a washcloth, bringing a clean set of clothes from the baby's drawer, lying

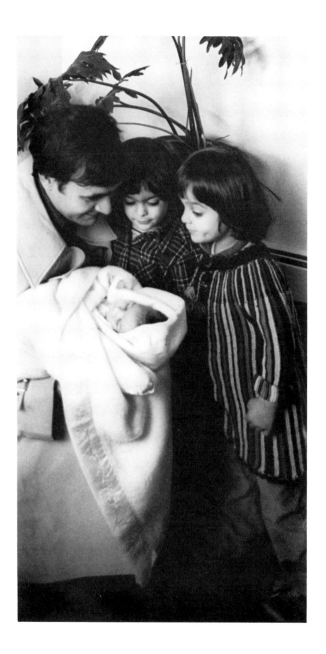

beside you and stroking the baby while you are nursing are some ways to make even the smallest children feel like an important part of this experience.

When you breastfeed, you are not just giving milk to your baby; it is almost as though you are giving your own substance. Since you do not hold back in any way, this can often be extremely exhausting. Most people do not realize the extent to which even a very healthy mother's energy is depleted by nursing.

In addition, your baby wakes you repeatedly and you find it difficult to get the rest you are missing. Discipline yourself in the first few weeks to nap whenever your baby naps, or at the very least, to nurse lying down so that you can relax, too. Lack of rest can prolong your recovery after childbirth.

Using lots of pillows to support your back and legs is the key to nursing lying down. Also, do not slide your arm under the baby's head. Just place your baby opposite your nipple, directly on the surface of the bed, and start the feeding. Burp gently after the baby has finished with the first breast (you will often have to change a diaper at this point, anyway), then offer the other breast. The baby usually drifts off to sleep and doesn't need to be moved to any other location. You can adjust a rolled towel at the baby's back to prevent the baby's rolling off the bed (a highly unlikely occurrence in the first three months, but some babies have done it!).

As you become comfortable with napping and nursing you may find that you, too, drift off to sleep along with your baby—even though you had planned to accomplish at least three or four things while the baby was asleep. They will still be there to do when you wake up. You deserve the nap. The baby usually sleeps more soundly when cuddled next to you, and you soon realize that you have become accustomed to the little grunts, snorts, sighs, and coughs that are typical of the very young baby. You sleep soundly, too, no longer worried about rolling over on top of the baby. Each of you knows exactly where the other is.

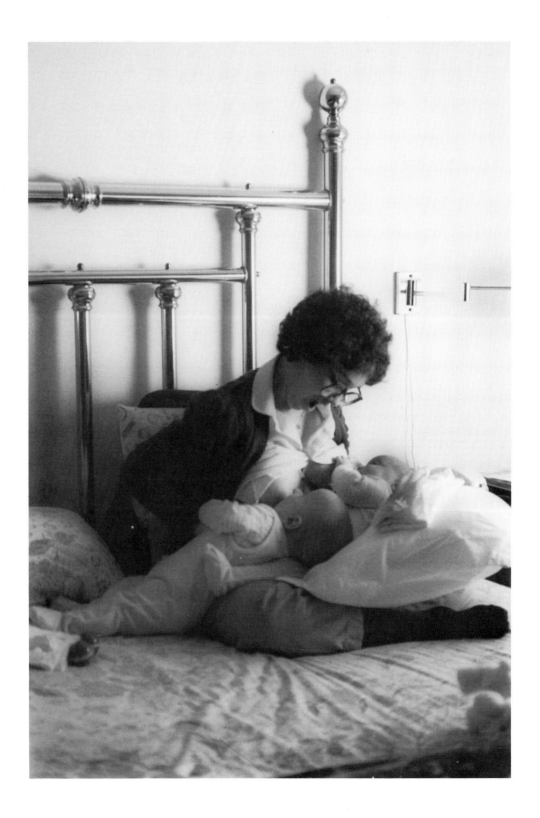

Relatives and other helpers leave eventually. Your mate returns to work, and now it is all up to you.

You may feel that since you are at home all day you should be able to manage the housekeeping, catch up on your correspondence, and breeze through the classic works of literature. After all, this should be almost like a vacation compared to the work schedule you have been used to, right? What a shock to find that you hardly have enough uninterrupted time to take a shower! If your one baby turned out to be twins, triplets, or more, you will of course find the work that much more multiplied. Your idyllic fantasies about crocheting little booties while the baby naps or coos contentedly in the nursery dissolve into the day-to-day reality of having to stop whatever else you are doing every hour or so to tend to the baby's physical needs—as well as emotional needs for simple companionship and play. A new baby is a full-time job. The immensity of your responsibility may bring you to tears as you feel intense pressure to get everything done.

Soon you realize that no matter what the state of the house, you must give top priority to relaxed nursings if you and the baby are to thrive as you should. If you have twins, you experiment with nursing them one at a time so that each has some personal time with you, or you find positions that are comfortable for nursing them simultaneously and use other times for individual play. No matter how busy you are, you keep up your excellent diet, eating a nutritious snack and having a beverage every time you nurse.

As the days pass, your baby spends more time awake. When babies are awake, they want to be with people— part of the family circle. So you work toward a new phase of baby care: the portable baby, that is, the baby who can go where you go, who is happiest when sharing the events of society at large. For the time being, this larger circle extends primarily to the members of your family and their at-home pursuits and activities. You develop skill in nursing your baby at times and in places that might not be the most tranquil, but this will pay off in a more contented baby who soon learns that the world is a dependable place and that your care can be trusted.

If you use your breast to comfort your baby even if you have just finished nursing ten minutes ago, you will not need a pacifier. Offering your breast to calm a crying baby who has just been startled by a sibling's loud laugh or a quick squabble over a game is appropriate. The baby will usually take the breast for a few minutes, calm down, then either go to sleep or look around once again for something interesting.

At the beginning of the second or third week at home you may notice that for a day or two your baby will want to nurse more often and will cry to be fed every hour. This is a sign that the baby is growing and needs more milk. The baby is not becoming spoiled by too much attention. The only way for you to make more milk is to have your breasts stimulated to produce it. Accommodate the baby. Refrain from substituting a pacifier, or your milk supply may fall behind the baby's genuine need.

Other than a rocking chair and a king-sized bed, the soft baby carrier turns out to be the most utilized item in your baby care layette. Even the tiniest baby can nestle comfortably in the slinglike folds, and this sort of carrier does not require anything to come between you and your baby, not even a layer of fabric. Not all carriers are designed so simply, and you may want to use the more complicated varieties later, but for ease of nursing while carrying the baby in it the sling-style works best.

This is invaluable when you must attend to a sudden development in the kitchen, for instance, and you do not want to rouse your baby, who is nearly asleep at your breast, because you'd like to sneak in a nap for yourself, too! With the baby still attached to your nipple, you can answer the telephone, turn down the flame under your sauce, check the muffins, and answer the back door buzzer. It's amazing how much can be accomplished with only one free arm!

You begin to suspect that your baby senses when it's mealtime and chooses just exactly the moment you sit down to eat to wake up.

You may resent this since you are hungry and would like to have a few moments to enjoy your meal and the rest of your family without having to settle the baby. Well-meaning friends may suggest just letting the baby cry it out, but you find the sound of your baby bawling so unnerving that you are unable to listen for more than a few moments without doing something about it. Also, the rest of the family finds it hard to converse or enjoy their food with the baby sounding like a siren in the next room. They expect you to take care of the situation with your breasts, and if the baby is hungry, this may be the best thing to do.

There are a few ways around this problem and you may switch game plans a few times a week so the baby does not always wind up on your lap every time you sit at the table for the next year. You may prefer to nurse while you eat once in a while, but being unable to butter your own bread for months on end can become a trial instead of a pleasant social experience.

It is very likely that your baby has missed some human contact if you have been busy working in the kitchen rather than "wearing" the baby in the carrier. Try to have a neighbor's child take the baby for a ride in the carriage, or have your mate put the baby in the carrier and both of them take a walk for a half hour before dinner. If you are lucky, the baby will sleep through at least part of the meal.

If you have the luxury of a flexible schedule, serve your main meal at midday or whenever your baby is most often napping (this is hard to predict in the early weeks). This can add a Continental touch to your weekends, anyway, and your "dinner" companions may find it amusing. Nurse after you eat, gather everyone together, and head for a matinée— the whole family can have a good time, and a quick something to eat before bed will satisfy appetites. Experiment with going to bed at 7 p.m. instead of midnight. After you wake at 1 a.m. and nurse the baby back to sleep, you and your mate may find the time is perfect for intimacy— something that is often hard to fit into your unpredictable days and nights. Try to look on the bright side and find ways to meet your baby's needs creatively. By adjusting some aspect of your daily routine, you may open up many new opportunities for enriching your life.

It is easier to give your attention to your other children or work associates when you know you are doing all you can to ensure your baby's well-being, physical and emotional.

It just seems to work out that the baby fits into most activities very easily when you are willing to offer your breast whenever your baby wants it. This is sometimes called "demand" feeding, but the terms "ad-lib," "self-regulated," "unrestricted," or "unlimited" breastfeeding are closer in spirit to the interaction that is taking place. The baby's needs are really quite straightforward: nourishment, warmth, appropriate stimulation. Breastfeeding provides all three, and it also ensures that your baby will have the close mothering that has characterized human relationships from the very beginning of our species. Your other children, your friends, relatives, and other associates will learn much from watching you with your baby.

When you decide you want to resume intercourse, check with your midwife or doctor to make sure that your stitches (if any) have healed and that your uterus has involuted, particularly if it is before the traditional six-week waiting period. Many women go for months after birth without a menstrual period when they are breast-feeding. However, this does not automatically mean that you are not ovulating. You could become pregnant before you ever have a period if you have intercourse just at the time you first ovulate. Breast-feeding ad lib around the clock does delay the return of menses for most women, but it is not a foolproof contraceptive. Research has shown that relying on ad-lib breastfeeding alone, with no other precautions against pregnancy being taken and frequent intercourse as the norm, results in children spaced approximately eighteen months apart.

If this is closer spacing than you would like, you will need to discuss your fertility with a counselor familiar with all the birth control methods available. Select a method that is compatible with your breastfeeding priorities: mucus assessment with ovulation charts and periods of abstention, foam *and* condom, or a diaphragm with contraceptive jelly or cream (because your internal dimensions may have changed, it is unwise to use your old diaphragm as it may no longer provide you with adequate protection). The birth control pill hormones affect the quantity and quality of your milk and the hormones are transferred to your baby. You may also be justifiably concerned about reports of their hazards to your health. The same worries may apply to the IUD, although if you have previously tolerated the device, it may continue to be your preference.

If your vagina seems loose—and this is usually the case—you need to resume your Kegel exercises (tightening and releasing all the muscles surrounding your perineal openings). Work on regaining the ability you had during pregnancy to stop and start your flow of urine at will. Extend your control upward inside the vaginal vault. Continue these exercises a few times a day for the rest of your life, for these are the muscles that support all your internal organs, including bladder and uterus.

If you seem to lack the vaginal lubrication you used to have, this may be due to hormonal changes caused by lactation. For now use a lubricant such as K-Y jelly. Your partner can put it on for you or you can apply it to his penis before entry.

The physical barriers to lovemaking may be easier to overcome than the emotional ones.

You may feel torn between your desire to be a perfectly accessible mother, available to your baby at all times, and your need to spend private time savoring your adult love relationship. You are sensitive to your mate's chagrin when he tells you about the jealous feelings he experiences from time to time toward his own child or his new perceptions of you as a mother (he may even identify you with his own mother and feel ambivalent about his sexual feelings for you). You feel that your body is still somewhat out of shape: sagging abdomen, heavy, leaking breasts that may gush at times of sexual arousal, extra weight from pregnancy that appears to have chosen all the wrong places to settle, an aching back from carrying the baby around so much. Who could want to make love to this, you wonder.

Still, you feel such tenderness at times toward everyone around you— and especially for your mate—that your affection must find some expression. Your other children, perhaps seeking some assurance of their place in your love circle, ask to climb into bed with you, their dad, and the new baby. You feel the warmth of having all those you care most about snuggled close, even if only for a short time. The new baby drops off to sleep after nursing. The older kids, feeling happy and secure, straggle back to their own beds. You and dad make a quiet exit to the living room or guest bedroom. You may be reminded of your first lovemaking experience. On the way down the hall, stop at the linen closet for a towel in case you need something for your dripping breasts.

Having a baby means you rarely get a full night's rest.

You may find it difficult to get back to sleep after late-night nursings, especially when you have been fully wakened. An occasional beer or glass of wine may be relaxing, but avoid the use of anything stronger or sleep-inducing drugs since everything you ingest appears in your milk.

You find that night nursing is more convenient when you, your baby, and your mate are all tucked into the same bed. The baby is less likely to wake up all the way since you hear the first lip-smacking that indicates the baby's readiness for a feeding. You roll over, offer the first breast, change the diaper (a dim nightlight is a help here) and dispose of it in a bedside container, then offer the second breast. No walking down the hall to satisfy a screaming, wide-awake infant!

Small muscle fibers around each nipple opening contract to hold the milk in and relax when the milk should be coming out. You hear your baby crying, and in preparation, these muscles release, your milk lets down, and your clothes are soaked. This may happen when you hear another baby, too.

You learn to recognize the tingly feeling that precedes the gush of milk and find that you can stop the shower by applying gentle pressure. You cross your arms in front of you and discreetly press your forearm against your breasts.

You try different types of bras to find the one that is the most comfortable. It may be a specially designed nursing bra with drop cups, a lightweight bra that can be pulled up or down easily, or if you are heavy-breasted, a very firm support bra. To provide additional pressure and an absorbent surface, place disposable pads (without plastic liners) or clean handkerchiefs (folded into squares) in the cups and change them when they get damp.

Remember that you are not just giving your baby your milk. You are giving your baby your undivided attention, your spirit, and a great deal of your reserve strength in these early weeks. You are making the transition from thinking of yourself as an individual to an individual with total responsibility for another person as well. Even if you are holding up well physically, you may find your emotions running rampant, and *that* wears you out by 8 p.m. every night! If you are starting to get cabin fever, think of joining an exercise class for new mothers and their babies, or at least visit a neighbor two or three times a week for a chat. You need adult companionship, no matter how much you love your baby. Total isolation at this time can lead to postpartum depression, too, so keep your channels of communication with other adults wide open. If you don't know anyone else who just had a baby, place a small ad in your local newspaper announcing a new mothers' group—and set the first meeting for your home. You will be pleased at the response and you may make a lifetime friend or two in the bargain.

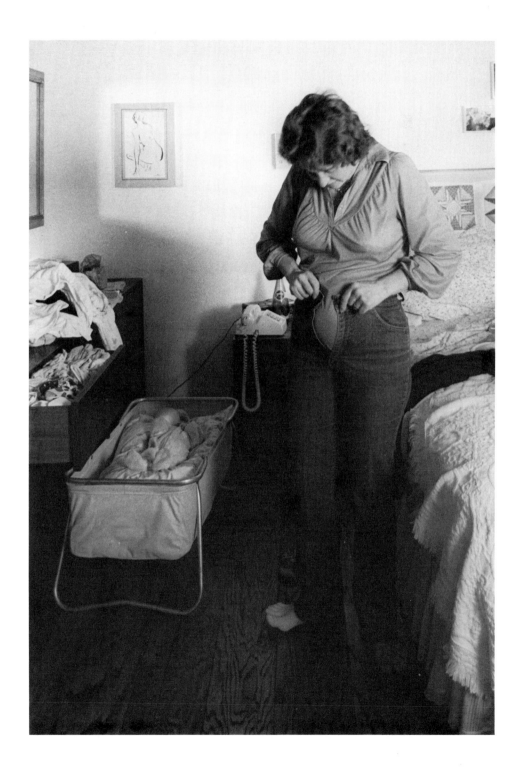

The day of reckoning is here: you've tried to get back into your favorite pair of jeans, and you can't make it. Your legs are too wide at the top, and the waistline appears to have been designed for somebody with a waist! Who was she?

On the scales, you see that you are still ten to twenty pounds or more over your prepregnancy weight. You've been trying to put this fact out of your head, but it now seems to be gaining in importance.

Put any ideas of crash diets out of your mind. Two or three days on a 1,200-calorie diet will spell the end of your milk supply. You cannot support lactation on your fat stores alone, although the stored calories you have left over from pregnancy are needed as part of your body's lactation effort.

Instead, continue your nursing mother's diet (the pregnancy diet, plus additional nutritious beverages or water) and avoid the temptation to snack on high-calorie, low-nutrition foods that are so convenient and so much a part of today's lifestyle. You need the best nutrition you can get to maintain the energy you need to mother well.

Force yourself to make time for some exercise every day. You are very busy, but you may not be getting the overall exercise you need. Your weight will gradually go down as your baby's goes up. Until your figure returns, you'll find elastic-waist pants and soft, full tops most comfortable—and most serviceable for nursing.

Your portable baby can accompany you almost anywhere. At first, you may feel embarrassed to nurse in public—or in mixed company. It is perfectly understandable to feel this way on a shrieking subway, perhaps. But you will at some time in the early weeks encounter a situation where you do not feel particularly threatened, where you are in the company of friends, and your baby wants to nurse. You might be in a restaurant, at the beach, in a store, in a taxicab, at a friend's house for an evening of cards, or at a relative's for a family celebration. So you do it. No fanfare. You just lift the front of your top with your free hand and guide the baby to the breast. Simple. Take along a lightweight shawl or baby blanket and you have a coverup. Most people won't even notice what you are doing, except for other women who have nursed—and they'll be all smiles.

Breastfeeding is a normal function of our female bodies. Your baby has a right to nourishment and to a place in society. People who are offended by the sight of a nursing baby and who express their feelings to you should be asked politely what is the basis of their reaction. Men commonly feel ambivalence because the female breast is so associated in our culture with a sexual availability that breastfeeding does not convey. Women who did not nurse may feel that you are needlessly displaying yourself. But your baby will appreciate it for what it is—a loving attention that only you can provide.

Traveling with your breastfeeding baby—even on long trips—is easy. No food bag to lug, no worry about heating formula or washing bottles or finding in the place you'll be visiting the kind of formula your baby tolerates. Your milk is always at the right temperature, always available, always digestible.

Your baby may really enjoy the motion of the car, train, boat, or plane. If it lulls your baby to sleep, you can lean back and relax for the entire trip, the baby resting on your chest or safely restrained in a car seat if you are driving.

When traveling by air, notify the airline ahead of time and they will try to save the seat next to you if the flight is not full. Putting the baby to the breast while the plane is making ascent and landing prevents unequal air pressure from hurting the baby's ears. Major airports have nursery facilities where you can rest, nurse, and change the baby if you have extra time between flights. These areas are usually much less crowded than the other restrooms as they are designated for families with babies only.

Your baby, who has been nursing well for the first three weeks, may suddenly start to cry for long periods of time, pull up the legs, and expel gas by mouth and/or rectum. If this happens, and nothing you do seems to make much difference to the baby's comfort, your baby probably has colic. It can happen to the breastfed as well as to the bottlefed infant, and most authorities blame the problem on an immature digestive system that fails to move foods through certain parts of the intestinal tract, causing pockets of gas to accumulate, with the attendant pain.

Colic can cause you seriously to question whether you are nursing properly, even though you seem to do nothing but rock and nurse constantly. Some babies have colic-like symptoms when they have an adverse reaction to a food taken by the mother, such as cow's milk and cow's milk products, coffee and other caffeine-containing beverages and foods (including chocolate), or anything that disagrees with the mother's own system. Milk intolerance can sometimes be overcome by the mother's using only boiled or evaporated milk in her diet; the heating deactivates the milk protein usually responsible for the upset. If cow's milk is the problem and using treated milk doesn't work, all forms of it must be completely removed from the diet: cheeses, yogurt, butter. It may take several days for the effects of this treatment to work.

Carry your baby, ask others to carry the baby, and take a nap yourself whenever you can. Colic exhausts everyone involved. Medication from your pediatrician may be the answer as a last resort. Colic ends, almost without exception, at about three months of age.

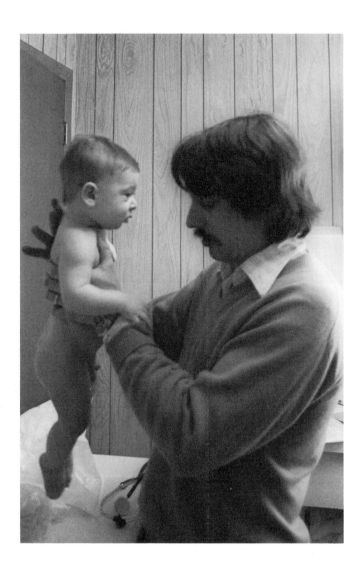

Your first visit with your baby's doctor or nurse-practitioner should come before the baby's birth. Issues about hospital care of your baby, attitudes about breastfeeding, and specifics of caring for your baby in the first month after birth can be discussed at this time. The health professional may suggest books to read, mothers' support groups to contact, or programs about parenting at area hospitals or clinics that you might find of interest.

Your baby may be examined by your doctor at the hospital shortly after birth or just before discharge. If your baby is born at home or at a birth center, part of your postnatal care should be to take the baby to the physician's office for evaluation within a day. Your next meeting with your baby's medical care provider is typically when the baby reaches one month of age, unless you have had some medical reason to bring the baby in sooner. You will continue to have regular appointments to check the baby's development throughout the next few years.

Your baby should have regained any weight lost after birth and added another pound or two by the one-month checkup. If your baby has not gained well, you need a complete evaluation to find out why. Supplemental feedings with formula only cut back on your baby's time at the breast, resulting in less milk for your baby. Your baby may have an ineffectual tongue action (flutter suck) that can be corrected. You may not be eating well enough for the life you are leading. A physician will take a complete medical history and do a physical examination of your baby to rule out metabolic disorders, infection, diarrhea, congenital heart disease, or abnormalities of the mouth, palate, and tongue. The physician will also examine the part you play in the breastfeeding process and will ask you about your diet, your let-down reflex, the condition of your breasts, and the general state of your health: whether you smoke or are taking any medication, and whether you have recently experienced any illness, psychological stress, or general fatigue that may be inhibiting your milk supply. Finally, you will be asked to nurse the baby so your interaction as a nursing couple can be observed.

Happily, almost all these problems have solutions. Your strong desire to breastfeed will make a great difference in seeing your baby through this phase and establishing a healthy, mutually satisfying breastfeeding experience. An outstanding reference for your doctor or health worker, most of which is also readable by the nonmedical professional, is *Breastfeeding: A Guide for the Medical Profession*, by Ruth Lawrence, M.D. (St. Louis: C. V. Mosby, 1980). This book gives detailed information about weight gain expectations in the breastfed baby and provides a step-by-step procedure for identifying and managing failure to thrive, as well as covering the full gamut of other problems that can crop up during breastfeeding.

Sometimes it is the mother who is ill. If you do not feel well, resist the urge to pretend that you are fine. Your mate can keep the household running while you cuddle up in bed and nurse the baby.

The baby has already been exposed to your germs, so you should not stop nursing. Antibodies produced by your body are passed on in your breast milk and provide protection.

When serious illness strikes a breastfeeding mother and hospitalization becomes necessary, breastfeeding may have to be postponed or even terminated. It is therefore unwise to neglect persistent symptoms of illness, since early diagnosis often leads to early cure, and a resumption of breastfeeding may then be possible.

If your baby catches a cold or even just has the sniffles, the consequences for breastfeeding are significant. The baby's nasal passages are tiny, and easily blocked by a small amount of mucus. The nasal passages are very close to the delicate ear canals, so a backup of mucus may trigger an ear infection in a small baby. If your baby seems to have a stuffy nose, nasal drops prescribed by your doctor or even just plain water dropped in with a medicine dropper can soften the mass so you can remove it with a nasal syringe from your drugstore. Nurse as soon as the baby's airway is clear, otherwise the baby will become frustrated at trying to breathe and suck at the same time and may end up frantically crying.

Even if you are able to remove a mass of mucus and clear the airway temporarily, the baby's membranes may be so swollen that mouth breathing is still necessary. In this case, the baby will latch on, suckle for ten to fifteen seconds, then break suction and take a few breaths. This will be repeated throughout the feeding until the baby is either full or exhausted. Usually either condition leads to slumber. Waking suddenly and crying immediately are signs of an ear infection in any child. Notify your pediatrician.

The most common illness in the nursing mother is mastitis or breast infection. The symptoms are fever, body aches, and a warm, painful reddish area on one or both breasts. Mastitis is usually preceded by a clogged milk duct, which is a milder form of the same disease and is treated in the same way.

The body's response to infection is to try to prevent its spread by walling off the affected area. When this occurs, the result is an abscess, which must be surgically drained. To avoid the need for surgical intervention, the infection should be treated promptly. Antibiotics may be necessary.

Keep both breasts as empty as possible by nursing as often as your baby is willing. The baby will not be harmed by nursing on the affected breast. Between nursings apply hot, moist compresses to the affected areas and gently massage the plugged duct, which may feel like a hard pea. A massage in a warm shower is a convenient way of combining both methods of treatment.

If you have had prior surgery on your breasts for chronic cystic changes or a biopsy of a suspicious lump, you are not automatically at higher risk for the development of mastitis during breastfeeding. In fact, nursing is often associated with a diminution of these breast problems because it stalls the recurrence of monthly hormonal swings associated with your menstrual cycle. As long as you are nursing you should maintain your regular program of breast self-examination even though your breasts are temporarily altered in size and possibly in texture. As always, report any changes to your physician.

All medications taken by a nursing mother pass through her milk, but most are considered to be of little risk to the baby because the quantities found in breast milk are so small.

Although no medication has been proven safe for your breastfed baby, the drug prescribed for you in a difficult situation may be less harmful to your baby than discontinuing breastfeeding.

Your pharmacist can provide you with copies of the information brochure the drug manufacturer must include with the product. Ask to have it included with your prescription so you can read it at home before you begin taking your medicine. Ask the pharmacist if the drug has any known side effects on the breastfed baby or any characteristics you should be aware of that might make you less responsive to your baby, such as drowsiness. If there is no alternative to this particular medication and it has powerful side effects, you may want to make arrangements for someone to come in and help with the baby while you take the course of treatment. If the drug is potentially harmful to your baby, you can pump your milk and discard it, temporarily using a prepared formula until you are able to nurse again.

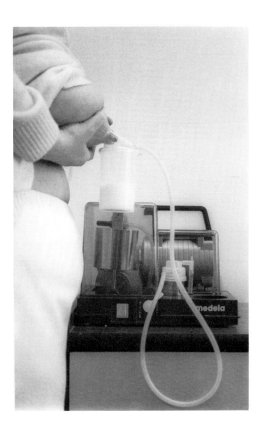

If you are too weak to express your milk by hand, or your hand expression technique takes too long, you may choose to use an electric pump. Many nursing mothers' groups rent pumps and give instructions for safe use. If you are hospitalized, the maternity service should be able to supply one if you are persistent in requesting it.

If you are using the electric pump to maintain your milk supply, try to pump at least every three hours.

If a breastfeeding mother must take toxic medication for an extended period of time, she may be forced to wean before either she or her baby is ready. Sudden, forced weaning presents potential problems for both members of the nursing couple.

Whenever there is a choice, weaning should be accomplished gradually for the good of mother and baby. The standard procedure is to replace one breastfeeding session at a time with a bottle or cup, depending on the baby's age and skill. Generally, if your baby is less than a year old, you will need to provide a formula rather than weaning directly onto cow's milk. Consult your pediatrician about replacement foods that satisfy the nutritional requirements for your baby's age group. Two days after replacing the first breastfeeding, replace another about twelve hours later than the time of the first bottle. Continue substituting bottles for the breast at two- to three-day intervals until nursing is terminated. If partial breastfeeding is desired, maintain the early-morning feeding and the late-night feeding or any other arrangement that suits your availability. Some breastfeeding is always preferable to no breastfeeding, particularly after your baby has become accustomed to your close companionship. Many mothers have breastfed part-time well into their child's second or third year when they and their babies continued to enjoy it.

If weaning is taking place on an emergency basis, the baby may refuse fluids for a period of days, but will often accept spoon feeding of diluted solids. Engorgement may cause the mother to experience a general malaise and other flu-like symptoms; "milk fever," as this is known, commonly lasts three to four days. Expression of milk, aspirin for pain, and ice packs for swelling are indicated. Both mother and baby may be depressed if breastfeeding has been a warm, satisfying experience, and the mother's sudden withdrawal from high levels of prolactin may trigger even greater feelings of sadness and loss. It helps to air your feelings and take pride in the amount of breastfeeding you were able to give to your baby. When you bottle-feed your baby, try to hold the baby close to your skin. This helps to relieve the feelings of loss for both of you.

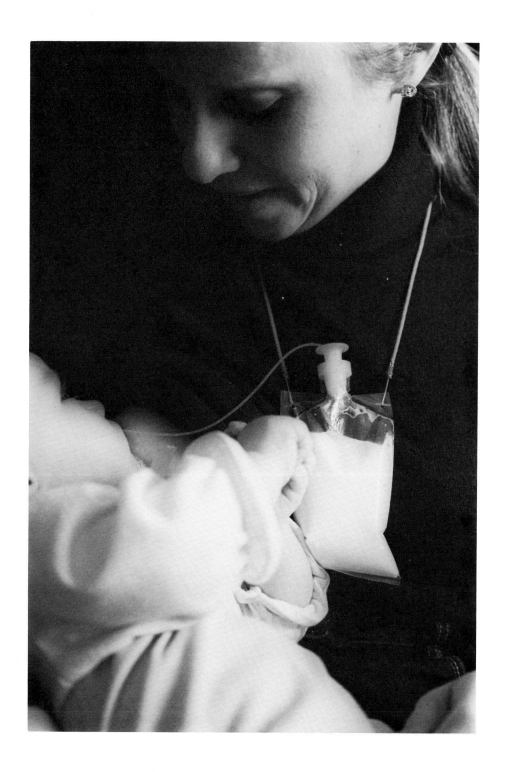

Although it is easiest to begin nursing right from birth, it is possible to regain your milk supply after a period of time without lactation. It is also possible to nurse an adopted baby, even if you have never been pregnant.

The Lact-Aid* is a nursing supplementer designed to help mothers establish their milk supply or when relactation is desired. The baby is put to the breast as often as possible to maximize stimulation. As the baby suckles, formula or donated breast milk flows through the tubing, which is taped alongside the nipple. In this way your baby is encouraged to keep suckling even though very little may be coming from the breast at first. The Lact-Aid kit comes with complete directions for its use, and the manufacturer also provides consultation by telephone or mail free of charge to anyone who has purchased it. Within three to four weeks' time most women will be able to satisfy some if not all of their babies' needs for breast milk. Of course, putting the baby to the breast provides emotional nourishment as well for both infant and mother, which is just as important as the milk itself. When full relactation does not occur, many mothers choose to use the breast as pacifier and rely on formula to ensure adequate nutritional intake.

*Available from: J. J. Avery, Inc., P.O. Box 6459, Denver, CO 80206.

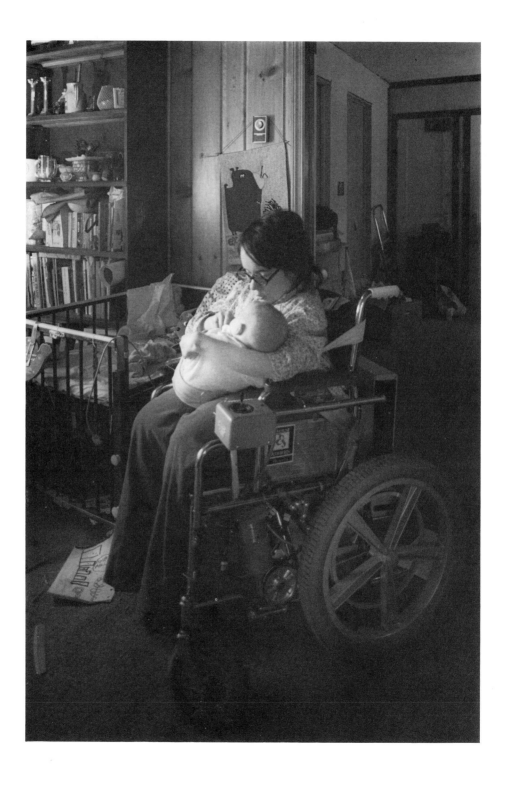

Mothers with disabilities must often be extraordinarily resourceful in arranging to take care of their infants themselves. Though discouraged in many cases from breastfeeding, a disabled mother may often feel that breastfeeding is something no one but she can do for her child. To facilitate her choice, she should contact the hospital where she is to give birth and explain to the nursing supervisor her particular disability and the kinds of services she will need to learn how to care for her baby. She may consult with nursery personnel, physical therapists, and her baby's doctor, as well as community services agencies to plan for home health aides or visiting nurses when she and the baby return home.

Disabled mothers who have successfully nursed encourage others who want to nurse to choose rooming-in during their hospital stay. In the supportive setting of the hospital, with a variety of helpers to provide backup and advice when needed, a mother in a wheelchair will be able to find out what her own capabilities are. She can determine the best height for a changing table and arrangement of supplies at home, for instance, and if she lacks upper body strength she can practice attaching her baby's carrier to her chair for extra support.

Disabled mothers recommend that there be a helper in the home for at least a month after childbirth. The purpose of the helper is to do things for the mother so that the mother can do as much as possible for the baby. For example, it is better to have a helper assist the mother out of bed so the mother can expend energy holding the baby, rather than have the helper soothe the baby.

If the mother has the use of only a single arm, nursing on one side at all times is possible. The breast not being nursed will become engorged initially, but since milk will not continue to be made if the breast is not suckled, this is a temporary problem.

Any disabled mother contemplating pregnancy or breastfeeding or with questions about any other aspects of mothering may contact a newly established clearinghouse and resource center staffed by mothers with disabilities: Evan Litty, Director, Disabled Parents United, 272 Orchard Road, Lake Secor, Mahopac, NY 10541, HOTLINE: 914-628-8248. The organization is most interested in collecting practical information and tips from disabled parents to share with others.

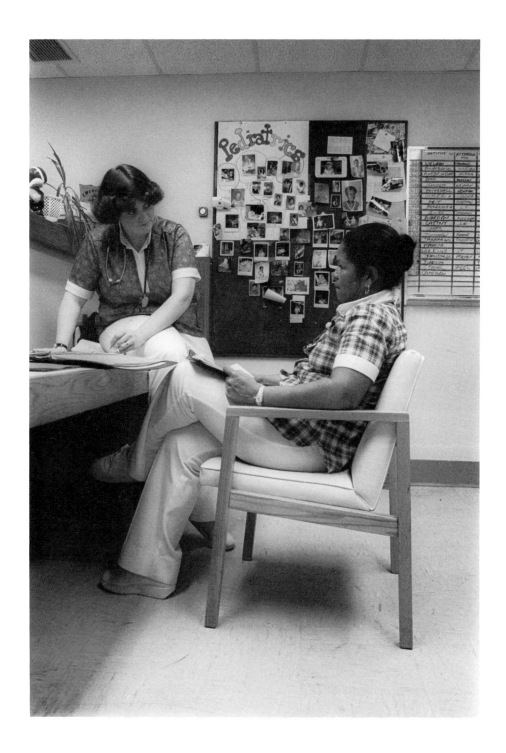

Choosing to return to work while your baby is still nursing does not mean you must wean.

You need to find someone who will care for your child in a way that is compatible with your philosophy of parenting. If your helper is sensitive to your desire to continue breast-feeding, the logistics of working and nursing are easier to handle.

If your helper can also do simple chores such as starting dinner, you will have more time to relax when you come home. You may find that part-time employment is the alternative that best satisfies your needs for career and motherhood. It is also possible, once your milk supply is established, to make a transition to part-time breastfeeding. That is, you nurse the baby often when you are together, including night nursings, and have the baby bottlefed formula by the helper when you are away. Many mothers who are the sole support of their families or whose income is essential to the family's welfare find this a workable solution to the dilemma of early weaning, a choice they do not relish. Some mothers are also able to express, either by hand or pump, enough milk to leave at home so that formula feedings are not necessary. If your baby is intolerant of formula and you must work, this is another option to explore.

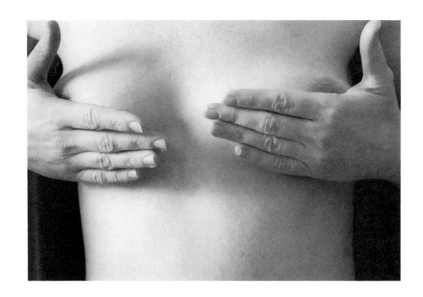

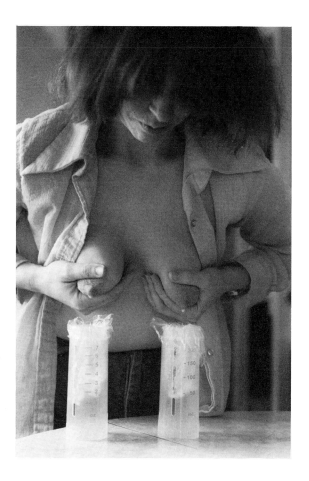

Whether or not you decide to return to employment outside the home while you are still nursing, it is a good idea to acquire the skill of hand expression. Your breastfeeding colleagues can assist you if you find the technique difficult at first.

Wash your hands and then start by gently massaging your breasts in whatever manner is most comfortable.

When you feel the milk letting down, squeeze the area just behind the areola rhythmically, using a scissorlike motion.

Since the milk lets down on both sides at the same time, it is quicker if you can express from both sides simultaneously.

Use any container you find convenient—a plastic bottle liner, a teacup, an old peanut butter jar—as long as it is clean and germ-free. Refrigerate or freeze the milk immediately. Refrigerated milk will keep for twenty-four hours, and milk that has been frozen must be used within a few hours after defrosting. Since it is not homogenized, it should be shaken before use.

It is in your employer's best interests to make concessions to your need to continue breastfeeding. The time spent in pumping milk for your baby is well invested, since breast milk helps ensure your baby's health. Most mothers stay home from work when their babies are sick, so any measure that reduces the incidence of baby illness is cost-effective for a business.

You may find a manual pump to be a useful alternative to hand expression. There are several models to choose from, the easiest being the type that has a detachable bottle for the milk to collect in. The "bicycle-horn" pump is the type most generally available, but, if used too vigorously, can lead to sore breasts and cracked nipples. If you must use a hand pump, this is how to do it so as to reduce the likelihood of any complications.

After sterilizing, attach the bottle to the pump device. Moisten the inside of the horn with water—this imitates the baby's saliva and provides lubrication. Massage your breast until you feel the let-down of milk. Then place the horn over your breast and squeeze the bulb rhythmically. The bulb need not be depressed completely; if it is uncomfortable, start by depressing the bulb only halfway. The milk collects in the bottle and can be refrigerated or frozen without additional handling.

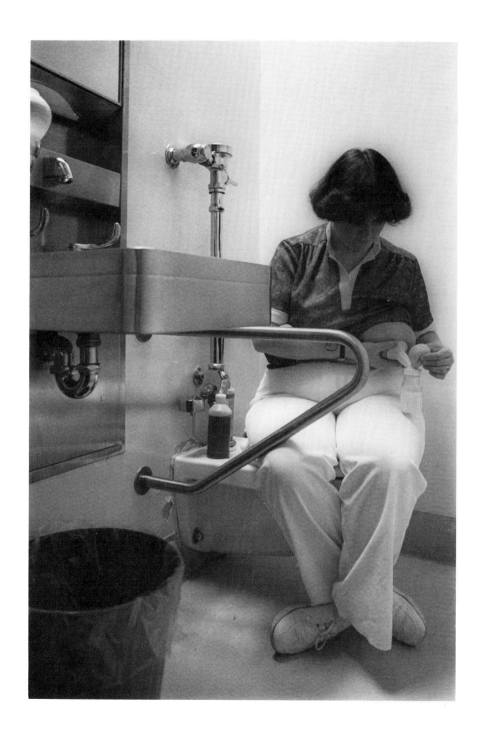

There may be other occasions in life when you have to decide whether to hire a babysitter, express some milk and go out alone, or take your baby along. Your choice may be influenced by such factors as convenience and cost (if the sitter is to be paid).

Whenever possible, try to arrange the times you must be away from your baby to coincide with times that your mate is available, so that he and your baby can develop their own relationship.

Your other children also have relationships to develop with their newest sibling. They express their feelings of jealousy by demanding your attention at the most inopportune times. You try to give each child some special time alone with you, but sometimes the day is too short and you are too tired.

If you find this happening often and your family life starts to suffer, it is time to talk about priorities. Is that trip, or meeting, or conference, or show, or party, or opening, or business luncheon really necessary? Could you accomplish the same thing with a phone call or letter? Is it time to change jobs? Can you delegate some of your work responsibilities or civic involvement to others for a period of time? Your baby is this dependent on you for only a short while, and you may be surprised to see how well your other children respond to only a few more minutes a day of your time. Don't feel guilty about your career goals. Carefully consider how to balance them with your goals as a mother and chart your course accordingly.

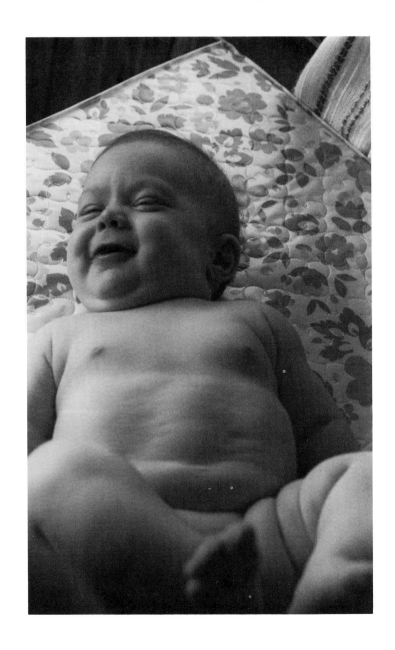

Your completely breastfed baby who has been put to the breast whenever crying, pacified with the breast when fussy, allowed to suckle until falling asleep, and nursed through the night for months is the epitome of wonderfully well-developed babyhood.

The baby stores extra fat in anticipation of the upcoming months when creeping, crawling, and eventually walking will demand large amounts of energy. If your baby is growing faster than your pediatrician's growth charts indicate is average, you may be advised to cut back on breastfeeding by substituting water for one feeding, by cutting back on the time allotted for nursing, or by forcing the baby to sleep through the night without nursing. It is important to know that these charts were devised years ago, primarily after weighing and measuring babies who were being bottlefed! They may have little relevance to your child who is obtaining the optimal nutrition possible.

You may worry that your chubby breastfed baby will stay that way for life. Again, the studies that have been done linking overweight babies to overweight in adulthood have been undertaken on babies who were fed artificially—bottle formulas and commercially prepared baby foods that, at the time of the studies, were heavily laden with extra starches and sugar. As long as your baby is being nourished by breast milk alone, you need not worry about a permanently fat child.

At around seven months, your baby's first tooth comes in. This may be preceded by several months of dribbling and drooling. If your baby's gums are swollen and nursing increases the discomfort, you may even have your nipples bitten.

If your baby is holding on to your nipple and pulling back, put your finger between the top and bottom gums and pry open the jaws. Since biting usually occurs toward the end of a nursing session, a firm "No!" and terminating that feeding immediately is usually sufficient to prevent recurrence.

Your pediatrician will recommend an analgesic for severe teething pain.

You may also find that your baby is easily distracted from nursing as interest grows in the world around. You can shield your baby's inquiring gaze with a shawl or other article of clothing, or—if all else fails—go into a quieter and perhaps darker room to finish the feeding.

Teething is one of the signs that tell you your baby is growing up. This is also the time when everything possible goes in the mouth. Once your baby is able to sit alone, both hands are free to grasp small objects.

Until now, nursing has provided the sole source of nutrition for your baby. Breast milk will continue to be important for a long time to come, but your baby is now ready for the addition of solid foods.

Start with a very little mashed banana, which is sweet and bland, like your milk. Offer the solid food first and then the breast. Introduce other unfamiliar tastes, one by one, waiting at least three days between new foods. After fruits, add cereals, meats, and vegetables, waiting until later to give eggs and cow's milk— among the most likely foods to cause allergy problems. All foods are put through a grinder or blender.

With the acquisition of motor skills—creeping, crawling, sitting, pulling up—your baby seems to develop a more playful personality. The repertoire of pats and strokes on your breast and face, the twisting of your hair round and round a pudgy hand, delight you and turn feedings into playtime.

When your baby is nursing without a diaper on, the baby may explore the genital area, just as has happened with all other parts of the body up until now. In an uncircumcised boy in particular, this natural activity may be helpful in loosening the foreskin, which is usually still somewhat adherent to the glans of his penis. As he matures, he will learn from you that this same motion is the first step in penile hygiene. Simple washing of the glans beneath the foreskin completes the procedure. At this age, babies have no conscious association of these body explorations with sexual activity, though they do seem to enjoy stroking (a baby's penis will become erect).

Exploration is important in other areas of your baby's life now, and you become alarmingly aware of new possible dangers—electrical outlets, pools, poisonous plants, unfamiliar animals. You marvel at how quickly your helpless infant has turned into a ready-for-anything toddler. You realize that your baby will continue to grow and that your protective feelings change with every new development.

"But if you nurse your baby ad lib, how will you ever enforce any discipline?" someone is bound to ask as your nursling gets to the age where having a mind of one's own seems crucial to a burgeoning sense of self-esteem.

Breastfeeding fosters a cooperative spirit on the part of mother and baby. Each is essential to the interchange. Neither wholly dictates the terms. It is a reciprocal act: we are doing something for each other, the partners seem to say. To breastfeed successfully requires a kind of discipline from both parties, an agreement, however unexpressed, to live up to your half of the bargain. This, it could be argued, goes to the heart of healthy human relationships, all of which, like breastfeeding, flower in an atmosphere of trust.

If slavish obedience to your every command is what your friend means by discipline, then no, it's highly unlikely that your breastfed child will appear disciplined to the world at large. Your requests will be met with whys. Your directives to play outside will be countered with an outstretched hand for you to come, too. You find yourself sharing bathtime. You have a curious helper every time you undertake a project, and if you should have to go elsewhere for a minute or two, you may return to find that your helper has completely taken over! While you may find it difficult to keep up, you have a child who feels secure enough to challenge the entire world because all the basic needs for love and personal attention have been met. This is not a failure of discipline. This is a triumph of self-confidence—one of the greatest gifts any parent can give a child.

Between the end of infancy and the beginning of toddlerhood, your baby develops different signals to communicate the desire to nurse. The pat on your breast, the tug on your clothing, the little hand playfully pulling on your bra strap, all say "Mama, I want to nurse."

This is a good time to reinforce the use of a private word that means nursing, so that you will not upset people who are shocked at the idea of breastfeeding a verbal child. Some popular euphemisms are "nummies," "emmy," "lala," and "nursy."

Your growing toddler gains new skills and explores new interests every day. You find yourself nursing while reading a story, nursing while playing "This Little Piggy Went to Market," and nursing while answering innumerable questions about

the way the world works.

After the shy period that most babies go through, your toddler is more sociable than ever. The fact that you are still a breastfeeding couple comes out in the conversations that your toddler has with others.

You begin to wonder if perhaps your baby is too old to nurse.

You may notice that you are larger on one side than the other. The older nursing baby often develops a preference and is difficult to dissuade.

There is no harm in one-sided breastfeeding, but try to switch breasts while letting your baby stay in the same position. If you are temporarily larger on one side than the other, realize that the larger breast will return to its former size when you stop breastfeeding.

As more and more of your child's total nutritional intake comes from foods shared by the whole family, you wonder if nursing is as essential as it was before.

While it is true that your child could survive without breast milk, the need for the emotional tie that breastfeeding strengthens will be present for a while. When at your breast, your older baby is between the womb and the world.

It is natural to want your baby to be the first in everything. You may feel disappointed if other women's babies sit up first, teethe earliest, or take the first step before your child does. In some circles, this competitiveness extends to weaning.

By now, your breastfeeding may have tapered off to a once or twice a day event—at naptime and at bedtime. And your child may seek you out for comfort from the breast when there's been a skinned knee, a fall down the stairs, or too high a push on the swing in the park.

Even though your child can hold a cup as well as your friend's child can, breastfeeding is still an important part of your relationship, too important to give up just yet.

Toddlerhood is a developmental transition. Not quite a baby, but not really a youngster yet, your toddler shakily stands somewhere between total dependence and emerging selfhood. You are your child's home base during this time of trial. When life gets too hectic for your toddler, you are there to provide the familiar emotional solace of the breast.

Sometimes it is inconvenient for you to nurse at just that moment, and your toddler understands about waiting for a few minutes. As you observe other children walking around with bottles, pacifiers, or thumbs in their mouths, to comfort themselves when life gets a little overwhelming, you sense anew the special closeness of breastfeeding.

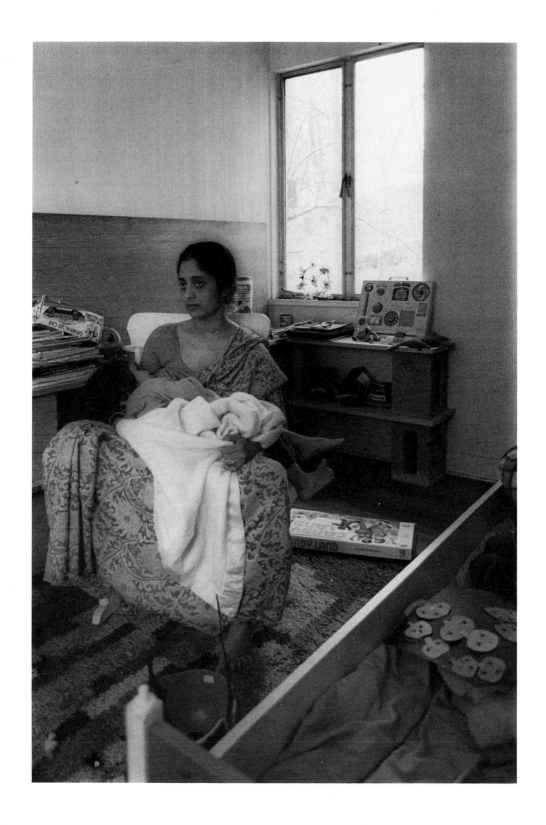

When your older child is ill, breast milk is part of the best medical care. It provides nourishment, antibodies, and fluid in nature's most easily digestible form. There is less danger of dehydration because even if your child refuses food and beverages, breastfeeding provides liquids and fills the ever-present need for comfort.

In case of severe illness which requires hospitalization, you insist on a medical facility that encourages parents to room in with their children. Recognizing that your sick baby needs you even more than usual, you refuse to wean abruptly.

You and your mate have been thinking and talking about expanding your family, but up until now it has all been abstract. Now you have the same sensations as last time, your breasts are even more tender, and you know that you are pregnant. You wonder if you will be able to love the new baby as much as you love your growing child.

Your appetite increases to meet the nutritional stress of simultaneous pregnancy and lactation. You slow down, spending more hours in restful contemplation. You ask yourself if it is time to wean, but your small nursing child shows no sign of being ready to stop.

During the middle months of your pregnancy, your child may tell you that the taste of your milk has changed, and you know that you are again producing colostrum. This is an opportunity to consider discontinuing breastfeeding this child, a negotiated end to this phase of your life together. It may be time to give the child a doll such as was done for you so many years ago. It is also time to invent new activities to do with this child—long walks, the library, a morning or two at nursery school (begin well before the new baby arrives so your older child does not feel displaced so acutely), a small play group—new interests that expand your child's range of contacts and encourage less dependence on you. Continue to tell your child in words and in actions of your deep and everlasting love. Stroke, fondle, hug, and kiss freely and often. You both need it and will continue to need it all your lives.

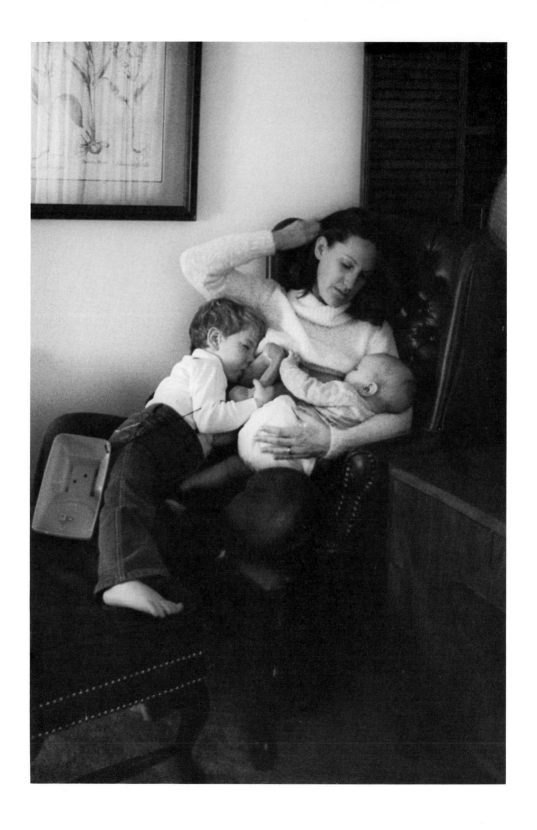

If you are expecting another child and your older child is not discouraged by the disappearance of the familiar taste of milk and becomes edgy or depressed when you try to wean, you know that the bond that keeps you together is more than just food. When your baby is born, colostrum is produced for another day or so and then gradually turns to mature milk again. You may attempt to wean the older child, but if you are not successful, you will find yourself nursing the old baby along with the new one.

Nursing two children together who are not twins is often called "tandem nursing." Each may choose a favorite breast, or you may alternate. It is important to feed the infant first, since the older child can ask for something from the refrigerator if there is not enough to go around. Seldom will the older child be nursing as often as the baby, though

the reappearance of milk after months of colostrum may encourage the older child to ask for it more often at first. As long as you eat enough, your breasts will provide enough milk for both nurslings. Sometimes the arrival of milk surprises the older child who has become fond of colostrum, and you find your weaning done for you: the older child rejects the milk and stops nursing at once!

If you find yourself becoming resentful of the fact that you seem to be doing nothing all day but nurse, you will have to force weaning. Resentment has no place in a breastfeeding relationship and your older child must not sense that nursing has become a contest of wills. Forcing the child to stop breast-feeding may hurt for a few days, but your anger at being forced to continue nursing will eventually hurt more.

It finally happens. Your child has
been growing up in many ways, and
the outside world beckons. Nursing
has become an occasional event. Then
one day you realize that it has been a
week since your child last asked to
nurse.

In allowing your child to decide
when to nurse, you have not imposed
society's idea of the proper time for
stopping. The security and self-
confidence developed during this
period of gradual weaning stay with
your child, just as the sensitivity to
human need that you have gained
will continue to enrich your life.

Appendix

Recommended Reading

Index

Appendix:
A Sound Diet for Pregnancy and Lactation

During pregnancy and lactation women need more of good quality foods than when they are not pregnant. To satisfy the nutritional stress of pregnancy and provide for her baby's growth, it is crucial for every mother to have, *every day,* at least:

1. One quart (four glasses) of milk: whole, low fat, skim, or powdered skim milk, or buttermilk. Natural cheese, yogurt, or cottage cheese can be used as substitutes for milk.

2. Two eggs.

3. Two servings of fish, chicken or turkey, lean beef, veal, lamb, pork, liver, or kidney. For each serving of meat, four ounces of cheese or six ounces of cottage cheese can be substituted.

Alternative means of obtaining complete proteins include the following combinations:*

· Brown rice with beans, cheese, seeds, or milk.

· Corn meal with beans, cheese, or milk.

· Beans with brown rice, whole grain noodles, or milk.

· Peanuts or peanut butter with sunflower seeds or milk.

· Whole wheat bread or noodles with beans, cheese, peanut butter, or milk.

*See *Diet for a Small Planet,* by Frances Moore Lappé (Ballantine Books, 1975).

4. Two servings of fresh, green leafy vegetables: mustard, beet, collard, dandelion, or turnip greens, spinach, cabbage, broccoli, parsley, kale, or Swiss chard.

5. Two choices from: a whole potato, large green pepper, grapefruit, orange, lemon, lime, papaya, or tomato. (One large glass of juice may be substituted for a piece of fruit.)

6. Five servings of whole grain breads, rolls, or cereals (such as granola). Other nutritious grains include wheat germ; oatmeal; buckwheat or whole-wheat pancakes or waffles; corn tortillas; corn bread; corn, bran, or whole-wheat muffins; and brown rice.

7. Three pats of butter or the equivalent in oil.

Also include in your diet:

8. A yellow or orange vegetable or fruit at least five times a week.

9. Liver once a week.

10. Salt: SALT YOUR FOOD TO TASTE.

11. Water: Drink to satisfy thirst.

12. Vitamin/mineral supplements. Supplementation should be used only as *insurance,* not as a substitute for foods.

This basic diet plan is the U.S. Department of Agriculture's basic four food groups adapted to the special needs of pregnant women.

When mothers follow this diet plan, they will be obtaining approximately 2,600 calories, at least 80 to 100 grams of high-quality proteins, and all other essential nutrients in amounts sufficient for pregnancy every day. It is important to note, however, that no two pregnant women have identical nutritional requirements. Women who are underweight, are experiencing undue stress, or were previously undernourished have even more pronounced nutritional needs during pregnancy.

The mother with twins has dramatically increased needs. She requires at least 30 grams more protein and 500 additional calories (which can easily be provided by an extra quart of milk per day or its equivalent in other complete proteins) above the normal pregnancy and lactation requirements.

It is of the utmost importance to keep in mind that no matter what medical problems are associated with pregnancy, the nutritional stress remains and *must be met every day.*

* SPUN sponsors a pregnancy nutrition hotline in North America: SPUN Nutrition/Toxemia Hotline, 914-271-6474

Recommended Reading

Avery, Jimmie Lynne. *Induced Lactation: A Guide for Counseling and Management.* Denver: Resources in Human Nurturing, International, P.O. Box 6861, 80206; 1979.

Brewer, Gail Sforza, and Presser (Greene), Janice, R.N. *Right from the Start: Meeting the Challenges of Mothering Your Unborn and Newborn Baby.* Emmaus, Pa.: Rodale Press, 1981.

Brewer, Gail Sforza, with Brewer, Thomas, M.D. *What Every Pregnant Woman Should Know: The Truth About Diets and Drugs in Pregnancy.* New York: Random House, 1977; New York: Penguin (paperback), 1979.

Brody, Lynne, M.D., and Parsons, Margot. "Breastfeeding: Completing the Maternity Cycle" in *The Pregnancy-After-30 Workbook,* Gail Sforza Brewer, ed. Emmaus, Pa.: Rodale Press, 1978.

Kippley, Sheila. *Breastfeeding and Natural Child Spacing.* New York: Penguin, 1975.

Lawrence, Ruth, M.D. *Breastfeeding: A Guide for the Medical Profession.* St. Louis: C. V. Mosby, 1980.

Liedloff, Jean. *The Continuum Concept.* New York: Alfred A. Knopf, 1977; New York: Warner Books (paperback), 1979.

Index

adoptive mothers, breastfeeding by, 97
afterpains from childbirth, 37
alcoholic beverages, intake of, by nursing
  mothers, 75
allergenic foods, 113
anesthesia, breastfeeding after, 51
areola. *See* nipples: areola

baby carriers, 64
bilirubin, excess of (jaundice), 49
birth control methods and breastfeeding,
  71
blood: circulation in breasts, 11; increase
  of, during pregnancy, 17; postpartum
  loss of, 37, 45
bottle feeding: attitudes toward, 20; of
  breast milk, 101, 103, 104, 107;
  formulas, 109; of water, 32; weaning
  to, 95
bowel movements of breast-fed babies, 31
brassieres, 15, 76; milk cups for, 13; tight,
  and sore nipples, 55
breastfeeding (*see also* nursing): attitudes
  toward, 19–20; by disabled mother, 99;
  energy depleted by, 58; in hospital.
  See hospitalization and breastfeeding;
  initiation of, 27–28, 97; of preemies,
  49; by pregnant mother, 129–30, 133;
  psychological benefits of, 35, 117;
  self-regulated, 67; of toddlers, 121; by
  working mother, 103
breast milk: antibodies in, 49, 89;
  artificially stimulated production of,
  97; digestibility of, 32–49; donors, 49;
  effect of medications on, 51, 93, 95;

fats in, 31, 43; flow of, 40; "fore" and
  "hind" milk, 31, 40, 43; let-down
  reflex, 40, 43, 76, 103, production of,
  31, 32, 40, 51, 62; storage of, 103, 104
breast pads, use of, 54, 76
breast pump, use of, 51, 54–55, 93, 101,
  104
breasts (*see also* nipples): change of, in
  nursing, 31, engorgement of, 32,
  52–54, 95; manipulation of, in
  nursing, 13; sensitivity of, in
  pregnancy, 7; size of, 7, 9, 10, 17;
  skin of, 11, stretch marks on, 11
burping, 35, 58

caffeinated beverages, intake by mother,
  84
Cesarean birth, 17, 43, 51
childbirth, 23; afterpains of, 37;
  contractions of, 37; hunger following,
  38; role of oxytocin in, 37, 40
children of family. *See* siblings
circumcision, 31
colic, 84
colostrum, 16, 52; antibodies in, 15;
  composition of, 15; first appearance of,
  10, 15; for preemies, 49; of pregnant
  nursing mother, 130, 133
contraceptives and breastfeeding, 71

demand feeding, 62, 66, 67, 69
depression: postnatal, 76; postweaning,
  95
diet for pregnancy and lactation, 138–39
disabled mothers, breastfeeding by, 99

A Note About the Authors

Janice Presser is a writer, editor, nurse-psychotherapist, and consultant, who has been active in the field of women's health and childbirth education for more than ten years. She lives with her husband and her two breastfed children in a 102-year-old Victorian house in Palmyra, New Jersey.

Gail Sforza Brewer, author of numerous books on pregnancy, nutrition, cuisine, and child care, is the mother of four breastfed babies. She lectures to professional and general audiences on these subjects and has been a consultant to international organizations interested in improving maternal and child health. She and her family live in Bedford Hills, New York.

JAMES S. WENZEL

A Note About the Photographer

Julianna FreeHand has received national recognition as a social historian. Although she has been taking pictures since the age of six, she did not commit herself to professional photography until her thirties. For some time her work has focused on conveying a woman's view of female reality. Married for sixteen years and mother of three breastfed children, she lives with her family in Croton-on-Hudson, New York.

A Note on the Photographs

The black and white photographs in this book were taken with Kodak's Tri-X and Infrared film mainly in New York State in Westchester, Putnam, and Dutchess counties, and the Bronx, and also in Yarmouth, Maine, and Fort Lee, New Jersey.

This book could never have been photographed using professional models. In order for it to be realized, one hundred and eight women, children, and men welcomed me within the privacy of their lives. The women, particularly, hoped to help other mothers breastfeed successfully. I thank them for sharing these intimate moments.

Helen Balgooyen, Joyce Bramwell, Dorothy Fanning, Armando Gellello, Barbara Hickernell, Melanie Hill, Mary Ellen Pileggi, Jean Rudah, and Phyllis Smith helped me find many of the people who appear in this book. Robbins Pharmacy in Croton-on-Hudson, Earthlight Foods in Yorktown Heights, Northern Westchester Hospital Center in Valhalla, and the Japanese American Society of New Jersey graciously allowed me to work on their premises. Dale Whitman and David Small provided me with valuable technical assistance.

—Julianna FreeHand

A Note on the Type

The text of this book was set, via computer-driven cathode ray tube, in Caledonia, a typeface designed by W. A. Dwiggins. It belongs to the family of printing types called "modern faces" by printers—a term used to mark the change in style of type letters that occurred in about 1800. Caledonia borders on the general design of Scotch Modern, but is more freely drawn than that letter.

Composition by the ComCom Division of The Haddon Craftsmen, Scranton, Pennsylvania. Printing and binding by The Murray Printing Company, Westford, Massachusetts.